COUNTRY COOKING

Ottenheimer Publishers, Inc.

Publisher: Sally Peters
Publication Manager: Diane B. Anderson
Senior Editor: Elaine Christiansen
Senior Food Editor: Jackie Sheehan
Test Kitchen Coordinator: Pat Peterson
Circulation Specialist: Karen Goodsell
Production Coordinator: Michele Warren
Publication Secretary: Mary Thell
Food Editor: Sharon Harding
Food Stylist: Sharon Harding
Food Stylist's Assistant: Mary Kay Sahli
Contributing Editor: Heather Randall King
Consulting Editor: William Monn
Home Economists: Pillsbury Publications
Nutrition Information: Pillsbury Technology
Design: Tad Ware & Company, Inc.
Photography: Studio 3

Cover Photo: Hearty Meatball and Vegetable Stew p. 46

Contents

Country Cooking

... with all conveniences for today's cooks plus delicious "extended-use" recipes

Country is in! Yes, indeed! Country furnishings, country music and especially country cooking. And just what is country cooking? Well, for one thing, it includes the best homemade foods you can recall from your culinary past. Grandma's tart apple pie with a tender crust that could melt away. Aunt Onie's sparkling preserves, which always graced the Sunday dinner table. And Mom's soothing homemade chicken soup, which often went to cheer a sick neighbor. One might say that country cooking is a potpourri of foods and recipes which are as satisfying to prepare as they are to eat. That was true years ago and it is every bit as true today with our recipes in **Country Cooking.**

This recipe collection, timed and tested to assist you in using autumnal fruits and vegetables at their peak, is a tasteful teaming of old and new, familiar and innovative. Preparation techniques feature favorite time-saving methods and appliances. The results? Practical, pleasing and popular foods. Ingredients star fresh-from-the-garden produce readily available at roadside stands and produce counters if not home-grown.

Perhaps the most appreciated fruits of fall are succulent and abundant apples, featured throughout this cookbook, and described in the desserts and snacks chapter.

> Another sure sign of this book's contemporary flavor is the accent on "extended-use" foods.

Call them "encores"; call them "planned-overs"—anything but "leftovers." The "new" look for "repeating performance" foods is one part creativity, one part technological advances. Instead of just heating up what's left as is, we produce imaginative salads, soups, potpies, sandwiches, casseroles and other mouth-watering mealmates. The freezer, microwave, wok, food processor and other reliable helps widen our choices in ways earlier cooks never dreamed possible.

Here are some tips for utilizing "extended-use" foods:

- Purchase larger cuts of meat in amounts suitable for the number of people to be served and number of meals you would like to have. In addition to weight, note amount of waste (fat and bone) before buying. Store uncooked meat in coldest part of refrigerator. Prepackaged meats can be stored in the original wrapping for 1 to 2 days. For longer storage, unwrap and cover meat loosely as some air helps retard bacteria growth.

- Cook meat as soon as possible after purchase and choose the best preparation method for each particular cut. Time carefully and use reliable doneness tests like a meat thermometer so meat will be tasty and tender.

- Meats can be frozen in original packaging for 1 to 2 weeks. For longer storage, over wrap or rewrap meat in moisture vapor-proof material and store in freezer at 0°F. or lower.

- Recipes in this cookbook assume that the meat is not frozen or has been defrosted. It is possible, however, to cook meat from the frozen state. Additional cooking time will be required. A meat thermometer, inserted after meat is thawed while cooking, can accurately indicate doneness.

- After the first use, prepare any remaining meat for "extended uses" to save time later and avoid waste. With a ham or turkey, for example, you may want to slice a portion for sandwiches, cube some for salads, potpies or casseroles, grind some for other uses or leave a portion in bulk for longer storage.

- Refrigerate cooked portions to be used within a day or so. Prepare any remaining portions by wrapping tightly in freezer wrap. Label and date each packet with contents and expected use, i.e., 2 turkey drumsticks for soup, 2 cups cubed ham for casserole, etc.

- Enliven "planned-overs" with appealing presentation and garnishes. Examples are soup toppers like Cheese Toppers from **Hearty Chicken Soup,** popcorn, finely chopped green onion or chives. Edible holders for salads, stews and chili include bread dough "bowls" like **Chili-in-a-Bowl,** taco or pastry shells, and cups of cabbage or lettuce.

COUNTRY COOKING

Main Dishes & Casseroles

Main Dishes & Casseroles

A new look for nostalgic cooking.

Who doesn't recall with relish wholesome, hearty dinners of one's childhood when the entire family was gathered around the table to pass heaping platters of Mom's homecooked specialties? But how many of us have the time to prepare these same marvelous menus on a daily basis? Must wonderful, warming favorites like chicken and biscuits, savory potpies with flaky crusts, pot roast teamed with vegetables and stuffed pork chops be only mouth-watering wishes?

No, indeed! The freshest produce of the season, convenience foods of highest quality, the latest appliances, modernized preparation techniques and reliably updated recipes like these found in **Country Cooking** mean that you can serve down-home favorites to your family as often as you like. And in a lot less time than did yesterday's cooks.

Because most of us cook by the calendar, this cooler time of year brings us enthusiastically back into the kitchen. It's a pleasure to warm the room with an aromatic oven-baked supper of slow-cooking roasts, hams and turkeys. Especially appropriate for weekend preparation, these larger cuts become delicious **"extended-use"** quick-to-fix meals for busy weekday suppers. Some combine with other ingredients like pasta, vegetables or rice for treasured one-dish delights like **Creamed Turkey in Noodle Ring**. Other transformations feature new looks like our **Ham and Corn Stuffed Potatoes** and speedy **Ham and Broccoli Skillet Supper.** Along with evoking pleasant memories, the enticing variations are as lively as they are likable.

Recipes in **Country Cooking** offer the delicious opportunity to savor the special flavors that come only from using fresh, quality ingredients and combining them carefully and reliably into memorable mainstays. The recipes here are for robust, family favorites that comfort and nourish—creative cooking for today's lifestyle.

Pictured on previous page, left to right: Turkey Breast with Cranberry-Nut Stuffing and Harvest Time Squash p. 64

This deliciously tempting way to serve turkey is perfect for those smaller families who want the traditional stuffed turkey. The sweet glaze enhances the meat.

Turkey Breast with Cranberry-Nut Stuffing

STUFFING

½ cup margarine or butter
½ cup chopped onion
¼ cup slivered almonds
4 cups herb-seasoned bread cubes
1 cup coarsely chopped cranberries
3 tablespoons sugar
2 tablespoons grated orange peel
½ cup orange juice

5 to 6-lb. fresh or frozen whole turkey breast with bone, thawed

GLAZE

¼ cup Citrus Marmalade (see Index) or orange marmalade
1 tablespoon margarine or butter, melted
¼ teaspoon ginger

Heat oven to 325°F. In large skillet, saute onion and almonds in ½ cup margarine until onion is tender. Stir in remaining stuffing ingredients; set aside.

Bone turkey breast (see Cook's Note).* Spread back of breast to open pockets. Spoon stuffing into pockets and down center of breast. Fasten with skewers. Place breast, skin side up, in roasting pan. Bake at 325°F. for 2 to 2½ hours or until temperature of thermometer inserted into thickest part of breast reaches 170°F.

In small bowl, combine all glaze ingredients. Brush over breast 2 or 3 times during last 30 minutes of baking. Slice to serve.
10 to 12 servings.

TIP: *If desired, breast can be baked with the bone in. Fill cavity with stuffing; cover with foil. Place, skin side up, in roasting pan. Bake and glaze as directed above. Carve from bone; spoon stuffing into bowl.

NUTRITION INFORMATION PER SERVING

SERVING SIZE: 1/12 OF RECIPE		PERCENT U.S. RDA PER SERVING	
CALORIES	360	PROTEIN	70%
PROTEIN	44g	VITAMIN A	6%
CARBOHYDRATE	19g	VITAMIN C	8%
FAT	12g	THIAMINE	4%
CHOLESTEROL	120mg	RIBOFLAVIN	10%
SODIUM	360mg	NIACIN	50%
POTASSIUM	470mg	CALCIUM	2%
		IRON	10%

COOK'S NOTE

To bone turkey breast, place turkey breast, skin side down, on counter. Insert a sharp knife at outside edge of ribs and work toward breastbone in center, cutting meat free and pulling it back in one piece as you cut. Do not cut through the skin. Repeat on the other side.

For your next turkey, we recommend this delicious sausage-apple stuffing, or substitute Bread Stuffing for Poultry for a more basic stuffing.

Roast Turkey with Sausage-Apple Stuffing

- ½ lb. bulk pork sausage
- ½ cup chopped onion
- ½ cup chopped celery
- 8 cups dry bread cubes
- 2 tablespoons finely chopped fresh parsley
- 2 teaspoons poultry seasoning
- 1 teaspoon salt
- ¼ teaspoon pepper
- ¼ cup margarine or butter, melted
- ½ cup water
- 2 cups chopped, peeled apples
- ⅔ cup raisins

8 to 24-lb. turkey

Heat oven to 325°F. In small skillet, brown pork sausage with onion and celery.

In large bowl, combine bread cubes, parsley, poultry seasoning, salt, pepper and margarine; mix well. Stir in water, apples, raisins and sausage mixture (including drippings).

Remove giblets from turkey. Rinse inside and out with cold water; pat dry with toweling. Spoon stuffing into turkey. Do not pack tightly. Close body cavity. Place stuffed turkey, breast side up, in roasting pan. Bake uncovered at 325°F. until internal temperature reaches 180°F. (See timetable.) Turkey is done when leg joint moves easily. Baste with drippings several times during baking. 8 to 18 servings.

Roasting Timetable

Weight	Baking time
8 to 12 lb.	3½ to 4½ hrs.
12 to 16 lb.	4½ to 5½ hrs.
16 to 20 lb.	5½ to 6½ hrs.
20 to 24 lb.	6½ to 7 hrs.

NUTRITION INFORMATION PER SERVING
SERVING SIZE:
1/18 OF RECIPE

		PERCENT U.S. RDA PER SERVING	
CALORIES	450	PROTEIN	120%
PROTEIN	79g	VITAMIN A	2%
CARBOHYDRATE	9g	VITAMIN C	2%
FAT	11g	THIAMINE	10%
CHOLESTEROL	260mg	RIBOFLAVIN	30%
SODIUM	420mg	NIACIN	70%
POTASSIUM	780mg	CALCIUM	6%
		IRON	30%

COOK'S NOTE

The Bread Stuffing for Poultry and the Sausage-Apple Stuffing will fill a 24-lb. turkey. For smaller turkeys, try heating your extra stuffing in a slow cooker while the turkey is baking. Measure remaining stuffing; spoon into slow cooker. Cover; set heat control on lowest setting. As turkey produces drippings, add 1 tablespoon drippings for each cup of stuffing; mix lightly. The stuffing from the slow cooker will be light and fluffy. The stuffing in the turkey will be more moist and compact.

Allow about ½ cup stuffing per pound of poultry. For a great tasting dressing, try heating extra stuffing in a slow cooker (see Cook's Note).

Bread Stuffing for Poultry

1 medium onion, chopped
2 stalks celery, chopped
½ cup margarine or butter
8 cups dry bread cubes*
2 tablespoons finely chopped fresh parsley, if desired
2 tablespoons poultry seasoning, sage or savory
1 teaspoon salt
¼ teaspoon pepper
   About ½ cup chicken broth or water

In large skillet, saute onion and celery in margarine until tender. In large bowl, combine bread cubes, parsley, poultry seasoning, salt and pepper; mix well. Add broth and margarine-onion mixture, stirring until desired moistness (stuffing will become a little more moist during cooking because it absorbs juices from bird).
18 (½-cup) servings.

TIP: *Day-old soft bread cubes can be substituted for dry bread cubes. Decrease broth to about ¼ cup.

NUTRITION INFORMATION PER SERVING
SERVING SIZE:
1/2 CUP

		PERCENT U.S. RDA PER SERVING	
CALORIES	120	PROTEIN	4%
PROTEIN	3g	VITAMIN A	4%
CARBOHYDRATE	14g	VITAMIN C	*
FAT	6g	THIAMINE	4%
CHOLESTEROL	0mg	RIBOFLAVIN	4%
SODIUM	330mg	NIACIN	4%
POTASSIUM	55mg	CALCIUM	2%
		IRON	4%

*Contains less than 2% of the U.S. RDA of this nutrient.

For an easy weeknight meal, stir together this mouth-watering down-home casserole. It's a good way to use that leftover turkey.

Turkey and Scalloped Potato Bake

1 pkg. Pillsbury Cheesy Scalloped Potatoes
2 cups cubed, cooked turkey or chicken*
2¼ cups water
1 cup shredded carrots
9-oz. pkg. Green Giant® Harvest Fresh® Frozen Sweet Peas
⅔ cup milk
2 tablespoons margarine or butter
4 oz. (1 cup) shredded Cheddar cheese

Heat oven to 400°F. Pour potato slices into ungreased 2-quart casserole. Sprinkle with contents of seasoning mix envelope and turkey. In medium saucepan, bring water to a boil. Stir in carrots, peas, milk and margarine; return to boil. Pour over potatoes; stir. Bake uncovered at 400°F. for 35 to 40 minutes or until potatoes are tender. Sprinkle with cheese. Bake an additional 3 minutes or until cheese is melted. 4 to 6 servings.

TIP: *Two cups cubed, cooked ham or 6 sliced, hard-cooked eggs can be substituted for turkey.

HIGH ALTITUDE—Above 3500 Feet: Bake uncovered at 400°F. for 40 to 45 minutes.

NUTRITION INFORMATION PER SERVING
SERVING SIZE:
1/6 OF RECIPE

		PERCENT U.S. RDA PER SERVING	
CALORIES	320	PROTEIN	35%
PROTEIN	24g	VITAMIN A	110%
CARBOHYDRATE	28g	VITAMIN C	6%
FAT	12g	THIAMINE	10%
CHOLESTEROL	70mg	RIBOFLAVIN	15%
SODIUM	690mg	NIACIN	20%
POTASSIUM	440mg	CALCIUM	25%
		IRON	10%

Quickest-Ever Turkey Potpie

15-oz. pkg. Pillsbury All Ready Pie Crusts
1 teaspoon flour
6 tablespoons margarine or butter
⅓ cup flour
¼ teaspoon marjoram
⅛ teaspoon pepper
1 cup milk
10½-oz. can condensed chicken broth
3 cups cubed, cooked turkey or chicken
16-oz. pkg. Green Giant® Frozen Mixed Vegetables, thawed*

Heat oven to 450°F. Allow 1 crust pouch to stand at room temperature for 15 to 20 minutes.** (Refrigerate remaining crust for later use.) Unfold pie crust; peel off top plastic sheet. Press out fold lines; sprinkle 1 teaspoon flour over crust. Turn crust, flour side down, on ungreased cookie sheet; peel off remaining plastic sheet. Invert 2-quart casserole over crust. With sharp knife, trace and cut around casserole rim; remove casserole. Trim an additional ¼ inch from edge of casserole-shaped crust. With cookie cutter or sharp knife, cut holes in crust. Cut additional shapes out of dough scraps, if desired; arrange over crust to decorate. Bake at 450°F. for 9 to 11 minutes or until light golden brown.

Meanwhile, in large saucepan, melt margarine. Stir in ⅓ cup flour, marjoram and pepper; cook until mixture is smooth and bubbly. Gradually add milk and chicken broth. Cook until mixture boils and thickens, stirring constantly. Stir in turkey and vegetables. Cook, stirring occasionally, until vegetables are tender, about 10 to 15 minutes. Spoon mixture into casserole; place baked crust on top. 6 servings.

TIPS: *For quick thawing, place unopened vegetable package in warm water for 20 minutes.
**Crust pouch can be brought to room temperature in microwave. Microwave one pouch on DEFROST for 20 to 40 seconds.

NUTRITION INFORMATION PER SERVING
SERVING SIZE:
1/6 OF RECIPE

		PERCENT U.S. RDA PER SERVING	
CALORIES	490	PROTEIN	45%
PROTEIN	28g	VITAMIN A	50%
CARBOHYDRATE	35g	VITAMIN C	6%
FAT	26g	THIAMINE	10%
CHOLESTEROL	70mg	RIBOFLAVIN	20%
SODIUM	760mg	NIACIN	30%
POTASSIUM	540mg	CALCIUM	8%
		IRON	15%

Grandma made hearty porcupine meatballs back in the '40s. Today's version substitutes ground turkey for ground beef. They still have the same great taste but with less fat and cholesterol.

Turkey Porcupines in Basil-Tomato Sauce

1 lb. ground turkey
½ cup uncooked rice
¼ cup finely chopped onion
½ teaspoon salt
¼ teaspoon pepper
2 tablespoons oil
2 teaspoons sugar
1 teaspoon basil leaves
1 cup water
2 (8-oz.) cans tomato sauce

In large bowl, combine turkey, rice, onion, salt and pepper; mix well. Shape into 16 balls. In medium skillet, lightly brown meatballs in oil, carefully turning to brown evenly. Stir in remaining ingredients; bring to boil. Reduce heat; cover and simmer 45 minutes, stirring occasionally. 4 servings.

NUTRITION INFORMATION PER SERVING
SERVING SIZE:
1/4 OF RECIPE

		PERCENT U.S. RDA PER SERVING	
CALORIES	380	PROTEIN	40%
PROTEIN	25g	VITAMIN A	25%
CARBOHYDRATE	30g	VITAMIN C	20%
FAT	18g	THIAMINE	15%
CHOLESTEROL	80mg	RIBOFLAVIN	20%
SODIUM	1050mg	NIACIN	35%
POTASSIUM	670mg	CALCIUM	6%
		IRON	20%

Quickest-Ever Turkey Potpie

Need a new idea for using that leftover turkey? This noodle ring with the creamy turkey and vegetable filling is special enough for company.

Creamed Turkey in Noodle Ring

RING

8 oz. (5 cups) uncooked wide egg noodles
⅓ cup chopped green onions
½ teaspoon salt
¼ teaspoon white pepper
¾ cup milk
1 tablespoon margarine or butter, softened
3 eggs, slightly beaten

FILLING

¼ cup margarine or butter, softened
¼ cup flour
1 chicken-flavor bouillon cube or 1 teaspoon chicken-flavor instant bouillon
⅛ teaspoon white pepper
2 cups milk
9-oz. pkg. Green Giant® Harvest Fresh® Frozen Cut Broccoli, thawed
1½ cups cubed, cooked turkey or chicken
2-oz. jar diced pimiento, drained

Heat oven to 350°F. Generously grease 6½-cup ring mold. Cook noodles to desired doneness as directed on package; drain. Stir in remaining ring ingredients; mix well. Spoon into prepared ring mold. Place mold in 13x9-inch pan; add hot water to depth of 1 inch. Bake at 350°F. for 45 minutes or until top is dry and mixture is set. Remove mold from water; let stand 10 minutes.

In medium saucepan, melt ¼ cup margarine. Stir in flour, chicken bouillon and ⅛ teaspoon white pepper; cook until mixture is smooth and bubbly. Gradually add 2 cups milk. Cook until mixture boils and thickens, stirring constantly. Add broccoli; cook over medium heat 10 minutes, stirring occasionally. Stir in turkey and pimiento; heat thoroughly.

Loosen edges of ring with spatula; invert onto serving platter with rim. Spoon filling into center of ring. 6 servings.

NUTRITION INFORMATION PER SERVING

SERVING SIZE: 1/6 OF RECIPE		PERCENT U.S. RDA PER SERVING	
CALORIES	420	PROTEIN	35%
PROTEIN	24g	VITAMIN A	20%
CARBOHYDRATE	40g	VITAMIN C	25%
FAT	17g	THIAMINE	30%
CHOLESTEROL	220mg	RIBOFLAVIN	30%
SODIUM	670mg	NIACIN	25%
POTASSIUM	430mg	CALCIUM	20%
		IRON	15%

When this juicy ham is prepared on Sunday, leftovers can be served during the week as Ham and Broccoli Skillet Supper, Ham and Corn Stuffed Potatoes or Ham Loaf with Peach Chutney (see Index).

Citrus Glazed Ham

4 to 5 lb. fully cooked boneless ham
½ cup Citrus Marmalade (see Index) or orange marmalade

Heat oven to 325°F. With sharp knife, score top of ham in crisscross pattern. Place in shallow roasting pan or 13x9-inch pan. Bake at 325°F. for 1½ hours or until thoroughly heated. During last 15 minutes of baking, brush ham with marmalade. 12 to 15 servings.

NUTRITION INFORMATION PER SERVING

SERVING SIZE: 1/15 OF RECIPE		PERCENT U.S. RDA PER SERVING	
CALORIES	250	PROTEIN	50%
PROTEIN	32g	VITAMIN A	*
CARBOHYDRATE	10g	VITAMIN C	40%
FAT	8g	THIAMINE	80%
CHOLESTEROL	80mg	RIBOFLAVIN	20%
SODIUM	1820mg	NIACIN	30%
POTASSIUM	440mg	CALCIUM	*
		IRON	10%

*Contains less than 2% of the U.S. RDA of this nutrient.

Prepare these substantial stuffed potatoes with "planned over" ham from the Citrus Glazed Ham (see Index). They are especially speedy to prepare in the microwave.

Ham and Corn Stuffed Potatoes

> 3 medium baking potatoes
> ¼ cup dairy sour cream
> 1 egg
> 1½ cups diced, cooked ham
> ¼ teaspoon pepper
>   Dash hot pepper sauce
> 12-oz. can Green Giant® Mexicorn® Whole Kernel Golden Sweet Corn with Green and Red Sweet Peppers, drained
> 2 oz. (½ cup) shredded Cheddar cheese

Heat oven to 350°F. Pierce potatoes with fork. Bake at 350°F. for 1 hour or until tender.

Slice each potato in half lengthwise. Holding each potato half in kitchen towel, carefully scoop out center, leaving ¼-inch shell. In large bowl, combine cooked potato, sour cream and egg; mix until smooth. Stir in ham, pepper, hot pepper sauce and corn. Spoon ⅙ of the mixture into each potato shell (skins will be very full and rounded); sprinkle with cheese. Place stuffed potatoes on ungreased cookie sheet. Return to oven and bake an additional 15 to 20 minutes or until thoroughly heated and cheese is melted. 6 servings.

■ MICROWAVE DIRECTIONS: Pierce potatoes with fork. Place in 8 or 9-inch square microwave-safe dish or on roasting rack. Microwave on HIGH for 7 minutes; turn potatoes and continue to microwave on HIGH for an additional 5 to 10 minutes or until tender.

Prepare potato mixture as directed above. Return stuffed potatoes to microwave-safe dish. Microwave on HIGH for 4 to 8 minutes or until thoroughly heated and cheese is melted.

NUTRITION INFORMATION PER SERVING

SERVING SIZE: 1/6 OF RECIPE		PERCENT U.S. RDA PER SERVING	
CALORIES	240	PROTEIN	20%
PROTEIN	14g	VITAMIN A	10%
CARBOHYDRATE	28g	VITAMIN C	25%
FAT	8g	THIAMINE	25%
CHOLESTEROL	80mg	RIBOFLAVIN	10%
SODIUM	670mg	NIACIN	15%
POTASSIUM	520mg	CALCIUM	8%
		IRON	6%

Chutney adds a special flavor to this traditional loaf.

Ham Loaf with Peach Chutney

> 1½ lb. (5 cups) cooked, ground ham
> 2 cups (3 to 4 slices) soft bread crumbs
> ¼ cup firmly packed brown sugar
> 2 tablespoons chopped green pepper
> 2 tablespoons chopped onion
> 1 tablespoon prepared mustard
> ¼ cup milk
> 2 eggs, beaten
> ¾ cup Microwave Peach Chutney (see Index) or mango chutney

Heat oven to 350°F. Grease 8x4 or 9x5-inch loaf pan. In large bowl, combine all ingredients except chutney; mix well. Press into prepared pan. Bake at 350°F. for 70 minutes or until center is set. Let stand 5 minutes.

In small saucepan, heat chutney over low heat until thoroughly heated. Invert ham loaf onto serving platter. Spoon chutney over loaf. 8 servings.

NUTRITION INFORMATION PER SERVING

SERVING SIZE: 1/8 OF RECIPE		PERCENT U.S. RDA PER SERVING	
CALORIES	240	PROTEIN	30%
PROTEIN	21g	VITAMIN A	4%
CARBOHYDRATE	24g	VITAMIN C	35%
FAT	7g	THIAMINE	45%
CHOLESTEROL	110mg	RIBOFLAVIN	15%
SODIUM	1130mg	NIACIN	20%
POTASSIUM	380mg	CALCIUM	4%
		IRON	15%

A creamy horseradish sauce is the perfect complement to this tender, juicy pot roast and succulent vegetables.

Pot Roast and Vegetables with Horseradish Sauce

       2 tablespoons oil
3 to 4 lb. beef chuck pot roast
     ½ teaspoon salt
     ¼ teaspoon pepper
       1 medium onion, sliced
    1½ cups water
       4 medium carrots, sliced
            lengthwise, cut into
            1½-inch pieces
       4 medium parsnips, cut into
            1½-inch pieces
       4 medium potatoes, quartered

SAUCE
     ½ cup whipping cream
     ¼ teaspoon salt
     ¼ teaspoon sugar
       2 tablespoons prepared
            horseradish
       1 teaspoon white wine vinegar

In Dutch oven, heat oil over medium-high heat; brown meat about 5 minutes on each side. Sprinkle with ½ teaspoon salt and pepper. Add onion and water. Cover; simmer 2 hours or until meat is tender. Add vegetables; cover and simmer 40 minutes or until vegetables are tender. Stir vegetables occasionally.

In small bowl, beat whipping cream, ¼ teaspoon salt and sugar until soft peaks form. Fold in horseradish and vinegar. Arrange meat and vegetables on serving platter; serve with sauce. 6 servings.

NUTRITION INFORMATION PER SERVING
SERVING SIZE:
1/6 OF RECIPE

		PERCENT U.S. RDA PER SERVING	
CALORIES	550	PROTEIN	70%
PROTEIN	44g	VITAMIN A	280%
CARBOHYDRATE	37g	VITAMIN C	40%
FAT	25g	THIAMINE	20%
CHOLESTEROL	150mg	RIBOFLAVIN	25%
SODIUM	370mg	NIACIN	45%
POTASSIUM	1320mg	CALCIUM	8%
		IRON	35%

Wait until you taste this red pepper sauce! The flavor and unique texture are quite different from more familiar tomato sauces.

Baked Stuffed Eggplant with Red Pepper Sauce

1 to 1¼ lb. eggplant, peeled
¼ cup milk
1 egg
1 cup cornflake crumbs
1 cup ricotta cheese
6 oz. (1½ cups) shredded Monterey jack cheese
¼ teaspoon basil leaves

SAUCE
2 red bell peppers, quartered
¼ cup oil
15-oz. can tomato sauce
1 teaspoon basil leaves
¼ teaspoon salt
Dash cayenne
1 garlic clove

🍴 FOOD PROCESSOR DIRECTIONS: Grease 15x10-inch jelly roll pan. With sharp knife, slice eggplant lengthwise into twelve ⅛-inch slices. In shallow bowl or pie pan, beat milk with egg. Dip eggplant in egg mixture, then in crumbs, turning to coat both sides. Arrange in single layer in prepared pan. Broil 4 to 6 inches from heat for 3 to 5 minutes or until tender and golden brown, turning once.

Heat oven to 350°F. In food processor bowl with metal blade or blender container, puree all sauce ingredients. Pour into ungreased 12x8-inch (2-quart) baking dish. In small bowl, combine cheeses and ¼ teaspoon basil. Spoon cheese mixture in ½-inch strip crosswise on each eggplant slice. Starting from shorter end, roll up.

Arrange rolls seam side down in sauce; cover. Bake at 350°F. for 30 minutes or until bubbly. Uncover; bake an additional 10 minutes. 6 servings.

Green pepper halves form the crust of this savory pie. It's a feast for the eyes as well as the appetite.

Stuffed Pepper Pie

2 quarts water
3 medium green peppers, halved, seeded
¼ cup finely chopped onion
1 cup water
2 tablespoons margarine or butter
1⅓ cups Hungry Jack® Mashed Potato Flakes
¼ cup milk
1 egg, slightly beaten
1 lb. bulk pork sausage, cooked, drained
1 medium tomato, cut into wedges
4 oz. (1 cup) shredded mozzarella cheese

In large saucepan, bring 2 quarts water to rolling boil. Place peppers in boiling water and cook for 15 minutes; drain. Arrange cut side up around sides of ungreased 8 or 9-inch pie pan.

Heat oven to 350°F. In same saucepan, combine onion, 1 cup water and margarine; heat to boiling. Remove from heat. Stir in potato flakes, milk and egg; mix well. Stir in pork sausage. Spoon into pepper-lined pie pan. Arrange tomato wedges on top; sprinkle with cheese. Bake at 350°F. for 15 to 20 minutes or until thoroughly heated and cheese is melted. 6 servings.

Stuffed Pepper Pie

The apple glaze adds moistness and mouth-watering flavor to these succulent homestyle pork chops.

Stuffed Apple-Glazed Pork Chops

2 slices raisin bread, toasted and cut into cubes (about 1 cup)
½ cup chopped apple
½ cup chopped pecans
¼ teaspoon grated orange peel
½ teaspoon salt
⅛ teaspoon cinnamon
 Dash pepper
¼ cup orange juice
4 pork chops, cut ¾ to 1-inch thick, with pockets

GLAZE
2 tablespoons sugar
1 tablespoon cornstarch
1 cup apple juice
2 tablespoons margarine or butter

Heat oven to 350°F. In medium bowl, combine bread cubes, apple, pecans, orange peel, salt, cinnamon and pepper. Stir in orange juice. Fill each pork chop pocket with ¼ of the stuffing mixture; place chops in 3x9-inch pan. Bake at 350°F. for 30 minutes.

Meanwhile, in small saucepan, combine sugar and cornstarch; stir in apple juice. Cook until mixture boils and thickens, stirring constantly. Remove from heat; stir in margarine. Pour evenly over pork chops. Bake an additional 30 to 35 minutes or until tender. 4 servings.

NUTRITION INFORMATION PER SERVING

SERVING SIZE: 1/4 OF RECIPE		PERCENT U.S. RDA PER SERVING	
CALORIES	450	PROTEIN	35%
PROTEIN	21g	VITAMIN A	6%
CARBOHYDRATE	32g	VITAMIN C	10%
FAT	26g	THIAMINE	50%
CHOLESTEROL	60mg	RIBOFLAVIN	20%
SODIUM	450mg	NIACIN	25%
POTASSIUM	480mg	CALCIUM	2%
		IRON	10%

Convenience foods combined with on-hand ingredients make this skillet dish a snap to prepare.

Ham and Broccoli Skillet Supper

3½ cups water
1 pkg. Pillsbury Tangy Au Gratin Potatoes
2 cups chopped fresh broccoli or 9-oz. pkg. Green Giant® Harvest Fresh® Frozen Cut Broccoli, thawed, drained
¼ cup chopped onion
¼ cup margarine or butter
1 cup diced, cooked ham
½ cup milk
5 eggs

In medium skillet, bring water to a boil; add potato slices. Reduce heat; cover and simmer 10 minutes. Add broccoli; cover and cook 5 minutes. Drain. Stir in onion and margarine. Saute 5 minutes, stirring occasionally. Stir in ham.

In small bowl, combine contents of seasoning mix envelope and milk; stir until smooth. Add eggs; mix well. Pour evenly over potato mixture in skillet. Cover and cook over low heat 20 to 30 minutes or until eggs are set. 6 servings.

HIGH ALTITUDE—Above 3500 Feet: Increase simmering time to 15 minutes.

NUTRITION INFORMATION PER SERVING

SERVING SIZE: 1/6 OF RECIPE		PERCENT U.S. RDA PER SERVING	
CALORIES	210	PROTEIN	20%
PROTEIN	12g	VITAMIN A	30%
CARBOHYDRATE	8g	VITAMIN C	40%
FAT	15g	THIAMINE	15%
CHOLESTEROL	240mg	RIBOFLAVIN	15%
SODIUM	540mg	NIACIN	6%
POTASSIUM	300mg	CALCIUM	8%
		IRON	8%

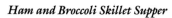

Ham and Broccoli Skillet Supper

 MAIN DISHES & CASSEROLES

Enjoy Down South goodness in this dinner for two.

Quick Jambalaya

10-oz. pkg. Green Giant® Rice Originals Frozen Rice Medley
3 slices bacon, crisply cooked, crumbled, reserving 1 tablespoon bacon drippings
¼ cup chopped celery
¼ cup chopped green pepper
¼ cup chopped onion
1 cup cooked shrimp
¼ to ½ teaspoon chili powder
2 tablespoons catsup
¼ teaspoon Worcestershire sauce

Cook rice as directed on package. In medium skillet, saute celery, green pepper and onion in reserved 1 tablespoon bacon drippings until celery is crisp-tender. Stir in bacon, cooked shrimp, chili powder, catsup, Worcestershire sauce and rice. Heat thoroughly. 2 servings.

■ MICROWAVE DIRECTIONS: Cook rice as directed on package. To cook bacon, place in shallow microwave-safe baking dish; microwave on HIGH for 4 minutes. Reserve 1 tablespoon drippings. In medium microwave-safe glass bowl, combine celery, green pepper, onion and reserved bacon drippings. Microwave on HIGH for 2 to 3 minutes or until celery is crisp-tender. Add bacon, cooked shrimp, chili powder, catsup, Worcestershire sauce and rice; microwave on HIGH for 4 to 5 minutes or until thoroughly heated.

NUTRITION INFORMATION PER SERVING

SERVING SIZE: 1/2 OF RECIPE		PERCENT U.S. RDA PER SERVING	
CALORIES	380	PROTEIN	35%
PROTEIN	21g	VITAMIN A	25%
CARBOHYDRATE	35g	VITAMIN C	45%
FAT	17g	THIAMINE	35%
CHOLESTEROL	100mg	RIBOFLAVIN	6%
SODIUM	790mg	NIACIN	30%
POTASSIUM	440mg	CALCIUM	8%
		IRON	25%

This hearty family dinner combines cornflake-coated chicken with tender biscuits, all in one pan.

Country Chicken and Biscuits

½ cup margarine or butter, melted
¼ teaspoon salt, if desired
¼ teaspoon pepper
⅛ teaspoon garlic powder
2½ to 3 lb. frying chicken, cut-up
1½ cups crushed cornflakes
7.5-oz. can Pillsbury Refrigerated Biscuits

Heat oven to 400°F. In shallow bowl, combine margarine, salt, pepper and garlic powder. Dip chicken pieces in margarine mixture, roll in cornflakes. Place chicken, skin side up, in ungreased 13x9-inch baking dish or pan. Bake at 400°F. for 40 to 50 minutes or until chicken is tender.

Remove from oven; drain. Move chicken pieces to one side of baking dish. Separate biscuit dough into 10 biscuits. Place in baking dish next to chicken. Return to oven and bake an additional 13 to 17 minutes or until biscuits are golden brown. 4 to 5 servings.

NUTRITION INFORMATION PER SERVING

SERVING SIZE: 1/5 OF RECIPE		PERCENT U.S. RDA PER SERVING	
CALORIES	460	PROTEIN	45%
PROTEIN	29g	VITAMIN A	20%
CARBOHYDRATE	26g	VITAMIN C	4%
FAT	26g	THIAMINE	20%
CHOLESTEROL	80mg	RIBOFLAVIN	20%
SODIUM	830mg	NIACIN	50%
POTASSIUM	440mg	CALCIUM	2%
		IRON	15%

Bow-tie pasta adds new appeal to tuna casserole.

Tempting Tuna Casserole

8 oz. (3½ cups) uncooked bow-tie pasta or wide egg noodles
2 tablespoons margarine or butter
½ cup chopped onion
½ cup chopped red or green bell pepper
3 tablespoons flour
¼ teaspoon salt
¼ teaspoon pepper
2 cups milk
1 cup water
1 chicken-flavor bouillon cube or 1 teaspoon chicken-flavor instant bouillon
¼ cup chopped green olives
2 (6½-oz.) cans tuna, drained
4½-oz. jar Green Giant® Sliced Mushrooms, drained Potato chips, crushed

Heat oven to 350°F. Cook pasta to desired doneness as directed on package. Drain; rinse with hot water. Set aside.

Grease 2-quart casserole. In large saucepan, saute onion and red pepper in margarine until tender. Stir in flour, salt and pepper; cook until mixture is smooth and bubbly. Gradually add milk, water and bouillon; bring to a boil, stirring constantly. Stir in olives, tuna and mushrooms. In prepared casserole, combine tuna mixture and pasta; sprinkle with potato chips. Bake at 350°F. for 30 minutes or until hot and bubbly. 4 (1½-cup) servings.

NUTRITION INFORMATION PER SERVING
SERVING SIZE:
1-1/2 CUPS

		PERCENT U.S. RDA PER SERVING	
CALORIES	540	PROTEIN	60%
PROTEIN	40g	VITAMIN A	35%
CARBOHYDRATE	59g	VITAMIN C	50%
FAT	15g	THIAMINE	45%
CHOLESTEROL	120mg	RIBOFLAVIN	35%
SODIUM	850mg	NIACIN	80%
POTASSIUM	740mg	CALCIUM	20%
		IRON	25%

Ordinary macaroni and cheese becomes extraordinary!

Three-Color Macaroni and Cheese

9 oz. (3 cups) tricolor spiral macaroni
¼ cup margarine or butter
¼ cup flour
½ teaspoon salt
⅛ teaspoon pepper
2½ cups milk
1 tablespoon prepared mustard
⅛ to ¼ teaspoon hot pepper sauce
4 oz. (1 cup) shredded Cheddar cheese
4 oz. (1 cup) shredded natural Swiss cheese
1 medium tomato, chopped, drained
¼ cup dry bread crumbs
1 tablespoon margarine or butter, melted

Heat oven to 375°F. In large saucepan, cook macaroni to desired doneness as directed on package. Drain; rinse with hot water. Set aside.

In same saucepan, melt ¼ cup margarine. Stir in flour, salt and pepper; cook until mixture is smooth and bubbly. Gradually add milk; stir in mustard and hot pepper sauce. Cook until mixture boils and thickens, stirring constantly. Add cheeses, stirring until melted. Carefully stir in tomato and cooked macaroni. Spoon into ungreased 2-quart casserole. Combine bread crumbs and melted margarine; sprinkle evenly over macaroni mixture. Bake at 375°F. for 20 minutes or until bubbly. 4 (1½-cup) servings.

NUTRITION INFORMATION PER SERVING
SERVING SIZE:
1-1/2 CUPS

		PERCENT U.S. RDA PER SERVING	
CALORIES	720	PROTEIN	45%
PROTEIN	30g	VITAMIN A	35%
CARBOHYDRATE	70g	VITAMIN C	6%
FAT	36g	THIAMINE	60%
CHOLESTEROL	70mg	RIBOFLAVIN	50%
SODIUM	880mg	NIACIN	30%
POTASSIUM	370mg	CALCIUM	70%
		IRON	20%

Serve these pancakes for a delicious change of pace. The sausage and apple filled pancakes are delicately seasoned with cinnamon and served with a tempting hot cider syrup.

Apple Sausage Pancakes with Cider Syrup

SYRUP
½ cup sugar
1 tablespoon cornstarch
⅛ teaspoon pumpkin-pie spice
1 cup apple cider or juice
1 tablespoon lemon juice
2 tablespoons margarine or butter

PANCAKES
1 egg
1 cup Hungry Jack® Buttermilk or Extra Lights® Pancake and Waffle Mix
⅔ cup milk
2 tablespoons oil
½ teaspoon cinnamon
½ cup shredded fresh apple
½ lb. bulk pork sausage, browned, drained

In medium saucepan, combine sugar, cornstarch and pumpkin-pie spice; stir in apple cider and lemon juice. Cook until mixture boils and thickens, stirring constantly. Remove from heat; stir in margarine. 1¼ cups syrup.

Heat griddle to 375°F. In small bowl, beat egg on high speed until thick and lemon colored, about 5 minutes. Lightly spoon pancake mix into measuring cup; level off. Add pancake mix, milk, oil and cinnamon. Fold in apple and sausage. Lightly grease griddle before baking each pancake. Pour a scant ¼ cup batter onto hot griddle. Bake until bubbles appear, about 2 minutes on each side. Serve with hot cider syrup.
3 to 4 servings.

HIGH ALTITUDE—Above 3500 Feet: No change.

NUTRITION INFORMATION PER SERVING
SERVING SIZE: 1/4 OF RECIPE		PERCENT U.S. RDA PER SERVING	
CALORIES	510	PROTEIN	15%
PROTEIN	11g	VITAMIN A	8%
CARBOHYDRATE	65g	VITAMIN C	4%
FAT	23g	THIAMINE	30%
CHOLESTEROL	90mg	RIBOFLAVIN	15%
SODIUM	960mg	NIACIN	10%
POTASSIUM	270mg	CALCIUM	10%
		IRON	10%

This easy and economical country-style oven meal is perfect family fare.

Country Pork and Kraut Supper

6 pork chops, cut ½-inch thick
2 tablespoons oil
1 medium onion, sliced, separated into rings
2 (16-oz.) cans sauerkraut, drained
2 red apples, sliced into wedges
2 tablespoons brown sugar
1 teaspoon caraway seed
1½ cups apple juice
⅛ teaspoon pepper
Paprika

Heat oven to 350°F. In large skillet, brown pork chops in oil; remove from skillet. Saute onion in drippings until tender. In ungreased 13x9-inch (3-quart) baking dish, combine sauerkraut, apples, brown sugar, caraway seed, apple juice and cooked onions. Place pork chops in sauerkraut mixture; sprinkle with pepper and paprika. Cover with foil. Bake at 350°F. for 1½ hours or until meat is tender. 6 servings.

NUTRITION INFORMATION PER SERVING
SERVING SIZE: 1/6 OF RECIPE		PERCENT U.S. RDA PER SERVING	
CALORIES	310	PROTEIN	30%
PROTEIN	20g	VITAMIN A	6%
CARBOHYDRATE	24g	VITAMIN C	20%
FAT	15g	THIAMINE	40%
CHOLESTEROL	60mg	RIBOFLAVIN	20%
SODIUM	780mg	NIACIN	20%
POTASSIUM	570mg	CALCIUM	6%
		IRON	10%

Pictured on previous page: Apple Sausage Pancakes with Cider Syrup

Shepherd's pie is a meat dish with a mashed potato "crust." For a new twist, this recipe uses mashed sweet potatoes. The spicy meat filling is the perfect complement.

Sweet 'n Spicy Shepherd's Pie

2 lb. (3 medium) sweet potatoes*
½ teaspoon salt
2 tablepoons margarine or butter

FILLING
1 lb. ground pork
1 cup chopped onions
2 garlic cloves, minced
1 teaspoon curry powder
½ teaspoon coriander
½ teaspoon salt
¼ teaspoon pepper
¼ teaspoon cinnamon
4-oz. can diced green chiles, drained
2 cups small cauliflower florets
1 cup frozen peas
¼ cup raisins
14½-oz. can tomatoes, undrained and chopped

In medium saucepan, cook sweet potatoes in boiling water until tender, about 40 to 45 minutes; drain. Peel and mash; stir in ½ teaspoon salt and margarine. Set aside.

Heat oven to 375°F. In large skillet, brown pork with onions and garlic; drain. Stir in spices and green chiles. Add remaining filling ingredients. Bring to a boil. Reduce heat; simmer uncovered 10 minutes, stirring occasionally. Spoon into ungreased 2-quart casserole. Spoon or pipe mashed sweet potato mixture over filling. Bake at 375°F. for 30 minutes or until edges are bubbly.
4 (1½-cup) servings.

TIP: *A 23-oz. can of sweet potatoes, drained, can be substituted for fresh sweet potatoes. Melt margarine before stirring into potatoes.

Extended-Use Recipe

A robust salad superbly seasoned with flavors reminiscent of the Orient.

Hearty Beef Salad

DRESSING
¼ cup oil
¼ cup red wine vinegar
2 tablespoons Dijon mustard
1 teaspoon soy sauce
½ teaspoon ginger
¼ teaspoon pepper
1 garlic clove, minced

SALAD
8 oz. (1½ cups) cooked roast beef, cut into strips
8-oz. can sliced water chestnuts, drained
4½-oz. jar Green Giant® Whole Mushrooms, drained
1 medium green pepper, cut into julienne strips
3 cups shredded cabbage

In small bowl or screw-top jar, combine all dressing ingredients; blend well.

In large bowl, combine beef, water chestnuts, mushrooms and green pepper. Pour dressing over beef-vegetable mixture; toss gently to coat. Cover; refrigerate 2 to 3 hours or until serving time. Just before serving, add cabbage; toss. Serve immediately.
4 servings.

Soups, Breads & Sandwiches

Soups, Breads & Sandwiches

Traditional, trendy and thrifty.

Often fall feasting focuses on wholesome, warm-from-the-oven breads, savory soups and stews and hearty, hit-the-spot sandwiches. In an era when much of life seems on fast-forward, leisurely breakfasts of French toast or relaxing suppers over steaming bowls of homemade soup seem like seldom-enjoyed luxuries.

However, we think you will want to take and make time to try these recipes. Many are quickly combined and microwaved or adapt well to make-ahead preparation. Still others, like **Pumpkin and Streusel Muffins** and **Hot Roll Wheat Batter Bread,** feature practical convenience products. And yes, some are the slow-cooking variety—wonderful for weekend preparation or other times when you can devote a few free hours to culinary artistry.

Our bread, muffin, biscuit and dumpling recipes are distinctively flavored, shaped and filled, incorporating some of America's innovative regional touches. And since it's quite obvious that sandwiches aren't just for lunch anymore, we offer a versatile array to satisfy hunger pangs around the clock.

There is a certain peace of mind for the cook who has a substantial kettle of soup, stew, chili or chowder simmering on the stove. One recipe can be the centerpiece for several meals and the mingled flavors combine with enticing aromas to welcome one and all to the harvest table. When there is no time for lengthy preparation, turn to recipes like **Carrot Orange Soup** and **Broccoli Lemon Soup**—two microwave favorites. **Harvest Pumpkin Corn Bisque** is another elegant but easy "quickie"—conventionally cooked but ready in minutes.

Because attractive appearance is important no matter what you are serving, we have added special presentation and garnishing tips so your food looks just as great as it tastes!

Pictured on previous page:
Chili-in-a-Bowl

This easily prepared batter bakes magically into a light and crispy bowl shape. The "bowl" is filled with thick and hearty chili.

Chili-in-a-Bowl

BOWL

- 1 tablespoon cornmeal
- ²⁄₃ cup water
- ¼ cup margarine or butter
- 1 cup Pillsbury's BEST® All Purpose or Unbleached Flour
- ¼ cup grated Parmesan cheese
- 1 tablespoon chili powder, if desired
- 2 teaspoons baking powder
- 4 eggs

CHILI

- 1 lb. ground beef
- 1 cup chopped onions
- 1 to 2 tablespoons chili powder
- 16-oz. can tomatoes, undrained, chopped
- 6-oz. can tomato paste
- 2 oz. (½ cup) shredded Cheddar cheese
- ½ cup dairy sour cream

Heat oven to 425°F. Grease 8 or 9-inch glass pie pan; sprinkle with cornmeal.* In medium saucepan, heat water and margarine to boiling. Lightly spoon flour into measuring cup; level off. Add flour, Parmesan cheese, 1 tablespoon chili powder and baking powder. Stir vigorously over low heat until mixture forms a ball; remove from heat. Beat in eggs, one at a time; continue beating until smooth. Spread evenly in prepared pan. Bake at 425°F. for 25 to 30 minutes or until center is firm and edge is golden brown. (A well will form in the center and the edge will puff up.) Make shallow slit on top surface of bottom crust to allow steam to escape. Cool 5 minutes. If desired, remove from pan and place on serving plate.

In large skillet, brown ground beef and onions; drain. Add 1 to 2 tablespoons chili powder, tomatoes and tomato paste. Simmer uncovered for 10 minutes, stirring occasionally. Serve in baked bowl. Top with Cheddar cheese and sour cream. 6 servings.

TIP: *For single serving bowls, six 10-oz. custard cups can be substituted for pie pan. Decrease bake time to 20 to 25 minutes. After baking, crack top of crusts in bowls to enlarge opening and allow steam to escape. Cool 5 minutes; remove from custard cups.

Bowls can be made up to 4 hours ahead. Let stand uncovered at room temperature.

HIGH ALTITUDE—Above 3500 Feet: Prepare 10-inch glass pie pan as directed above. Increase water to ¾ cup. Decrease flour to ¾ cup. Omit baking powder.

NUTRITION INFORMATION PER SERVING			
SERVING SIZE:		PERCENT U.S. RDA	
1/6 OF RECIPE		PER SERVING	
CALORIES	520	PROTEIN	40%
PROTEIN	27g	VITAMIN A	70%
CARBOHYDRATE	31g	VITAMIN C	35%
FAT	32g	THIAMINE	20%
CHOLESTEROL	260mg	RIBOFLAVIN	30%
SODIUM	800mg	NIACIN	30%
POTASSIUM	810mg	CALCIUM	30%
		IRON	30%

COUNTRY COOKING

Appetites will determine how to slice this fun party sandwich.

Sloppy Joe-by-the-Inch

1½ lb. ground beef
1 medium onion, sliced, separated into rings
½ teaspoon salt
⅛ teaspoon pepper
2 tablespoons prepared mustard
8-oz. can tomato sauce
6-oz. can tomato paste
14 to 22-inch loaf French or Italian bread, unsliced*
Quick Pickles (see Index) or sliced pickles

In large skillet, brown ground beef and onion; drain well. Stir in salt, pepper, mustard, tomato sauce and tomato paste. Simmer uncovered for 10 minutes.

Cut bread loaf in half lengthwise. Place halves cut side up on ungreased cookie sheet. Broil 2 to 4 minutes or until lightly toasted. Spoon beef mixture onto bottom half of loaf; top with pickles. Replace top half of loaf. To serve, cut into desired lengths. 6 to 8 servings.

TIP: *Thin French baguettes are not recommended. Three to four-inch wide loaves work best. Two shorter loaves can be substituted for one long loaf.

NUTRITION INFORMATION PER SERVING

SERVING SIZE: 1/8 OF RECIPE		PERCENT U.S. RDA PER SERVING	
CALORIES	480	PROTEIN	40%
PROTEIN	24g	VITAMIN A	15%
CARBOHYDRATE	59g	VITAMIN C	20%
FAT	15g	THIAMINE	30%
CHOLESTEROL	60mg	RIBOFLAVIN	25%
SODIUM	1210mg	NIACIN	35%
POTASSIUM	610mg	CALCIUM	6%
		IRON	30%

This popular all-American favorite has a new twist. The chili is topped off with a colorful ring of shoe peg corn and spicy green chiles.

Spicy Shoe Peg Chili

1 lb. ground beef
1 medium onion, chopped
1 stalk celery, chopped
1 tablespoon chili powder
16-oz. can tomatoes, undrained, chopped
8-oz. can tomato sauce
½ cup water
2 cups Green Giant® Frozen White Shoe Peg Corn
4-oz. can chopped green chiles, drained*
Tomato wedges, if desired

In medium skillet, brown ground beef with onion and celery; drain. Stir in chili powder, tomatoes and tomato sauce. Simmer until thoroughly heated, stirring occasionally.

In small saucepan, bring water to boil. Add corn; bring to second boil. Stir; cover and reduce heat. Simmer 3 to 5 minutes or until thoroughly heated; drain. Stir in chiles. To serve, spoon beef mixture into shallow bowl or onto serving platter with rim. Spoon corn mixture to form ring around top of beef mixture. Garnish with tomato wedges. 4 servings.

TIP: *If a less spicy flavor is desired, use ½ can green chiles.

NUTRITION INFORMATION PER SERVING

SERVING SIZE: 1/4 OF RECIPE		PERCENT U.S. RDA PER SERVING	
CALORIES	390	PROTEIN	35%
PROTEIN	24g	VITAMIN A	100%
CARBOHYDRATE	32g	VITAMIN C	60%
FAT	18g	THIAMINE	15%
CHOLESTEROL	80mg	RIBOFLAVIN	20%
SODIUM	860mg	NIACIN	35%
POTASSIUM	1040mg	CALCIUM	6%
		IRON	25%

Pictured top to bottom: Cereal Balls p. 85 and Sloppy Joe-by-the-Inch

Homemade chicken soup, hearty and nutritious, is a great way to warm up on cool fall nights. We think you'll have fun being creative with the Cheese Topper shapes.

Hearty Chicken Soup with Cheese Toppers

3½ lb. whole frying chicken
7 cups water
1½ teaspoons salt
½ teaspoon thyme
⅛ teaspoon pepper
1 large (1 cup) onion, chopped
3 bay leaves
3 celery stalks, sliced into ½-inch pieces
2 cups Green Giant® Frozen Cauliflower Florets (from 16-oz. pkg.)
1 cup Green Giant® Frozen Sweet Peas (from 16-oz. pkg.)
1 cup julienne-cut carrots

CHEESE TOPPERS
      Pie Crust Cut-Outs (see Index)
      Grated American cheese

In Dutch oven, combine chicken, water, salt, thyme, pepper, onion and bay leaves. Bring to a boil. Reduce heat; cover and simmer 1 hour or until chicken is tender. Remove chicken from broth; let cool slightly. Discard bay leaves, skin and bones from chicken.* Cut chicken into pieces. Skim fat from broth. Add celery to broth; bring to a boil. Reduce heat; cover and simmer 5 minutes. Add cauliflower, peas, carrots and chicken; bring to a boil. Reduce heat; cover and simmer 12 minutes or until vegetables are tender.

Prepare Pie Crust Cut-Outs, sprinkling them with American cheese. Garnish each serving with Cheese Toppers. 7 (1½-cup) servings.

TIP: *Recipe can be prepared up to this point 1 day ahead and refrigerated. Lift fat from broth. Continue as directed above.

NUTRITION INFORMATION PER SERVING
SERVING SIZE: 1-1/2 CUPS

		PERCENT U.S. RDA PER SERVING	
CALORIES	330	PROTEIN	40%
PROTEIN	25g	VITAMIN A	100%
CARBOHYDRATE	24g	VITAMIN C	30%
FAT	14g	THIAMINE	10%
CHOLESTEROL	74mg	RIBOFLAVIN	10%
SODIUM	750mg	NIACIN	40%
POTASSIUM	480mg	CALCIUM	6%
		IRON	10%

A bisque is a cream soup of pureed vegetables. In this recipe, the flavors of corn and pumpkin perfectly complement one another.

Harvest Pumpkin Corn Bisque

10-oz. pkg. Green Giant® Niblets® Corn Frozen in Butter Sauce, thawed
¼ cup sliced green onions
1 tablespoon sugar
⅛ teaspoon cinnamon
16-oz. can (2 cups) pumpkin
10½-oz. can condensed chicken broth
2 cups half-and-half
Lime slices

In medium saucepan, heat corn in butter sauce and onions until thoroughly heated, stirring occasionally. Stir in sugar, cinnamon, pumpkin and chicken broth; blend well. Bring to a boil, stirring frequently. Reduce heat; cover and simmer 5 minutes. Stir in half-and-half. Heat gently, stirring frequently. DO NOT BOIL. Garnish with lime slices. 6 (1-cup) servings.

NUTRITION INFORMATION PER SERVING
SERVING SIZE: 1 CUP

		PERCENT U.S. RDA PER SERVING	
CALORIES	210	PROTEIN	10%
PROTEIN	7g	VITAMIN A	340%
CARBOHYDRATE	20g	VITAMIN C	10%
FAT	11g	THIAMINE	4%
CHOLESTEROL	30mg	RIBOFLAVIN	10%
SODIUM	640mg	NIACIN	8%
POTASSIUM	430mg	CALCIUM	10%
		IRON	8%

Hearty Chicken Soup with Cheese Toppers

When my great-grandma prepared stew, it was always topped with dumplings. In this recipe, those same delicious dumplings are formed into an eye-appealing lattice shape. The stew is great without dumplings, too.

Beef Stew with Dumpling Lattice

STEW

2	tablespoons oil
1½	lb. boneless beef stew meat, cut into 1½-inch cubes
1	teaspoon dry mustard
1	teaspoon marjoram
½	teaspoon salt
¼	teaspoon pepper
1	garlic clove, minced
1	bay leaf
4	cups water
10½-oz.	can condensed beef broth
2	cups cubed rutabaga or 2 carrots, sliced
2	stalks celery, cut into 1-inch pieces
1	medium potato, peeled and cubed
1	medium green pepper, cut into 1-inch pieces
1	medium onion, cut into 1-inch pieces

DUMPLINGS

1½	cups Pillsbury's BEST® All Purpose or Unbleached Flour
2	tablespoons finely chopped parsley
2	teaspoons baking powder
½	teaspoon salt
⅓	cup shortening
6 to 7	tablespoons cold water
¼	cup flour
¼	cup cold water

In Dutch oven, heat oil over medium-high heat; brown meat in hot oil. Stir in dry mustard, marjoram, ½ teaspoon salt, pepper, garlic and bay leaf. Add 4 cups water and beef broth; bring to a boil. Reduce heat; cover and simmer 1½ hours or until meat is tender. Discard bay leaf. Add vegetables; return to boil. Cover and simmer 10 minutes.

Meanwhile, lightly spoon 1½ cups flour into measuring cup; level off. In medium bowl, combine 1½ cups flour, parsley, baking powder and ½ teaspoon salt. Cut in shortening with pastry blender or fork until consistency of coarse meal. Add 6 to 7 tablespoons cold water; stir with fork until mixture leaves sides of bowl and forms a ball. Turn onto floured surface; gently knead 5 to 6 times. Roll to ⅛-inch thickness; cut into 1-inch wide strips.

In small bowl, combine ¼ cup flour and ¼ cup cold water; mix well. Stir into stew until thickened and bubbly. Arrange dough strips lattice-fashion over hot, bubbling stew. Cover; cook over medium heat for 25 minutes or until dumplings are fluffy. 6 servings.

HIGH ALTITUDE—Above 3500 Feet: It may be necessary to add an additional 1 to 2 tablespoons water to dumpling dough.

NUTRITION INFORMATION PER SERVING
SERVING SIZE:
1/6 OF RECIPE

		PERCENT U.S. RDA PER SERVING	
CALORIES	500	PROTEIN	45%
PROTEIN	30g	VITAMIN A	4%
CARBOHYDRATE	40g	VITAMIN C	50%
FAT	24g	THIAMINE	25%
CHOLESTEROL	70mg	RIBOFLAVIN	20%
SODIUM	770mg	NIACIN	35%
POTASSIUM	670mg	CALCIUM	10%
		IRON	30%

These buns are a flavorful alternative to plain hamburger buns and so easy to make with Hot Roll Mix.

Corn Buns

16-oz. pkg. Pillsbury Hot Roll Mix
- ½ cup cornmeal
- 2 tablespoons sugar
- 1¼ cups hot tap water (110 to 120°F.)
- ¼ cup finely chopped green pepper
- 2 tablespoons margarine or butter, softened
- 1 egg
- 1 teaspoon water
- 1 egg

In large bowl, combine flour mixture with yeast from foil packet, cornmeal and sugar; mix well. Stir in 1¼ cups hot water, green pepper, margarine and 1 egg until dough pulls away from sides of bowl. Turn dough out onto lightly floured surface. With greased or floured hands, shape dough into a ball. Knead dough for 5 minutes or until smooth. If necessary, sprinkle flour over surface to reduce stickiness. Cover dough with large bowl; let rest 5 minutes.

Grease large cookie sheet. Divide dough into 8 equal pieces; shape into balls and flatten slightly. Place on prepared cookie sheet; cover completely with towel. Let dough rise 20 minutes on cookie sheet set over large pan to which hot water has been added.

Heat oven to 375°F. In small bowl, beat 1 teaspoon water and 1 egg; brush over buns. Bake at 375°F. for 13 to 15 minutes or until golden brown. 8 buns.

HIGH ALTITUDE—Above 3500 Feet: No change.

NUTRITION INFORMATION PER SERVING
SERVING SIZE:
1 BUN

		PERCENT U.S. RDA PER SERVING	
CALORIES	290	PROTEIN	15%
PROTEIN	9g	VITAMIN A	4%
CARBOHYDRATE	51g	VITAMIN C	6%
FAT	5g	THIAMINE	25%
CHOLESTEROL	70mg	RIBOFLAVIN	20%
SODIUM	440mg	NIACIN	20%
POTASSIUM	125mg	CALCIUM	2%
		IRON	10%

This hearty sandwich filling has excellent flavor and is especially outstanding with Corn Buns.

Barbecued Beef Sandwich Filling

- 4 cups shredded, cooked beef
- ¼ cup firmly packed brown sugar
- 1 tablespoon dry mustard
- ¼ teaspoon pepper
- 1½ cups water
- ¼ cup vinegar
- ¼ cup margarine or butter
- ½ teaspoon salt
- 1 cup catsup
- 1 tablespoon Worcestershire sauce
- 8 Corn Buns or hamburger buns

In large skillet, combine beef, brown sugar, mustard, pepper, water, vinegar and margarine. Bring to a boil. Cover; reduce heat and simmer 20 minutes. Add salt, catsup and Worcestershire. Simmer uncovered 20 to 25 minutes or until desired consistency. Serve on sliced Corn Buns. 8 (½-cup) servings.

NUTRITION INFORMATION PER SERVING
SERVING SIZE:
1/2 CUP

		PERCENT U.S. RDA PER SERVING	
CALORIES	540	PROTEIN	45%
PROTEIN	28g	VITAMIN A	20%
CARBOHYDRATE	67g	VITAMIN C	10%
FAT	17g	THIAMINE	35%
CHOLESTEROL	130mg	RIBOFLAVIN	30%
SODIUM	1060mg	NIACIN	40%
POTASSIUM	490mg	CALCIUM	4%
		IRON	30%

COUNTRY COOKING

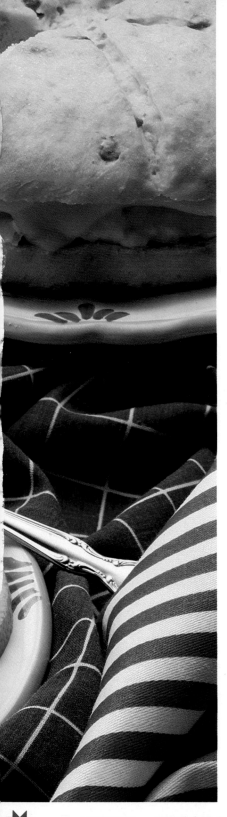

One giant sandwich makes eight tasty breakfast sandwich wedges. It's an easy breakfast idea for overnight guests.

Breakfast in a Biscuit

Bacon Biscuit Wedges, page 38
2 tablespoons margarine or butter
4 eggs, beaten
1 medium tomato, sliced
4 oz. (4 slices) American cheese

In medium skillet, melt margarine while Bacon Biscuit Wedges are baking. Add eggs; cook over medium heat until eggs are set, stirring occasionally.

Slice biscuit in half horizontally, leaving bottom half on cookie sheet. Spoon eggs onto bottom half of biscuit. Arrange tomato over eggs; top with cheese. Replace top half of biscuit. Return to oven; bake at 400°F. for 5 to 7 minutes or until cheese begins to melt. To serve, cut into wedges. 8 servings.

NUTRITION INFORMATION PER SERVING

SERVING SIZE: 1/8 OF RECIPE		PERCENT U.S. RDA PER SERVING	
CALORIES	340	PROTEIN	20%
PROTEIN	12g	VITAMIN A	10%
CARBOHYDRATE	27g	VITAMIN C	4%
FAT	21g	THIAMINE	20%
CHOLESTEROL	160mg	RIBOFLAVIN	20%
SODIUM	570mg	NIACIN	10%
POTASSIUM	180mg	CALCIUM	20%
		IRON	10%

Biscuits are a wonderful southern tradition. This easy-to-make version is flavored with bacon and cut into wedges. For the most tender biscuits, knead the dough as little as possible.

Bacon Biscuit Wedges

2 cups Pillsbury's BEST® All Purpose or Unbleached Flour
¼ cup (about 4 slices) crumbled, cooked bacon
2 teaspoons baking powder
½ teaspoon salt
¼ cup shortening
⅔ to 1 cup milk
1 tablespoon margarine or butter, melted

Heat oven to 400°F. Grease cookie sheet. Lightly spoon flour into measuring cup; level off. In large bowl, combine flour, bacon, baking powder and salt. Cut in shortening with pastry blender or fork until consistency of coarse meal. Add milk; stir with fork until mixture leaves sides of bowl and forms a soft, moist dough. Turn onto floured surface; gently knead 5 or 6 times or until no longer sticky. Shape dough into ball. Place on prepared cookie sheet; flatten into 8-inch circle. With sharp knife, score top surface into 8 wedges. Bake at 400°F. for 21 to 26 minutes or until golden brown. Brush with melted margarine. Cut into wedges to serve. 8 biscuit wedges.

HIGH ALTITUDE—Above 3500 Feet: No change.

NUTRITION INFORMATION PER SERVING

SERVING SIZE: 1/8 OF RECIPE		PERCENT U.S. RDA PER SERVING	
CALORIES	220	PROTEIN	8%
PROTEIN	5g	VITAMIN A	2%
CARBOHYDRATE	25g	VITAMIN C	*
FAT	10g	THIAMINE	15%
CHOLESTEROL	4mg	RIBOFLAVIN	10%
SODIUM	300mg	NIACIN	10%
POTASSIUM	95mg	CALCIUM	8%
		IRON	8%

*Contains less than 2% of the U.S. RDA of this nutrient.

Pumpkin and spices make the difference in these great-tasting, quick muffins from a mix.

Pumpkin and Streusel Muffins

MUFFINS

16.6-oz. pkg. Pillsbury Nut Quick Bread Mix
⅓ cup raisins
¾ teaspoon cinnamon
¼ teaspoon nutmeg
¾ cup canned pumpkin
½ cup milk
¼ cup oil
1 egg

TOPPING

2 tablespoons flour
2 tablespoons brown sugar
½ teaspoon cinnamon
1 tablespoon margarine or butter
1 tablespoon chopped nuts

Heat oven to 375°F. Grease bottoms only of 12 muffin cups. In large bowl, combine all muffin ingredients; stir 50 to 75 strokes until dry particles are moistened, breaking up any lumps. Divide batter evenly among prepared muffin cups.

In small bowl, combine flour, brown sugar and ½ teaspoon cinnamon. Cut in margarine with pastry blender or fork until consistency of coarse meal; stir in nuts. Sprinkle mixture evenly over muffin batter. Bake at 375°F. for 20 to 22 minutes or until toothpick inserted in center comes out clean. Remove from pan immediately. Serve warm or cool. 12 muffins.

MICROWAVE DIRECTIONS: Prepare muffin batter as directed above. Using 6-cup microwave-safe muffin pan, line each cup with 2 paper baking cups to absorb moisture during baking. Fill cups ⅔ to ¾ full. Prepare topping and sprinkle over muffin batter as directed above. Microwave on HIGH for 2½ to 3½ minutes or until toothpick inserted in center comes out clean, rotating pan once halfway through baking. Remove muffins from pan and discard **outer**

paper baking cups immediately. Cool 1 minute before serving. Repeat with remaining batter. 17 muffins.

HIGH ALTITUDE—Above 3500 Feet: Add 1 tablespoon flour to dry mix.

Tired of the same old breakfast menus? Surprise your family with these delicious and different breakfast sandwiches.

French Toast with Sausage and Apple Butter

12-oz. pkg. bulk pork sausage
  2 tablespoons margarine or butter
  2 tablespoons milk
  3 eggs
  8 slices raisin bread
  ¼ cup Microwave Apple Butter (see Index) or apple butter
     Powdered sugar, if desired

Form pork sausage into 4 patties; cook as directed on package.

In large skillet, melt 1 tablespoon margarine over medium heat. In shallow bowl or pie pan, beat milk with eggs. Dip 4 slices bread in egg mixture, turning to coat both sides. Fry in skillet over medium heat about 3 to 4 minutes on each side or until golden brown. Repeat with remaining 1 tablespoon margarine and 4 slices bread. Spread 1 tablespoon apple butter on 4 French toasts; top with sausage patty and second French toast. Sprinkle with powdered sugar. 4 servings.

Mmm! You'll love the flavor of the pepper jelly baked inside the apple corn muffins.

Apple Corn Muffins with Pepper Jelly

  2 cups Pillsbury's BEST® All Purpose or Unbleached Flour
  ½ cup cornmeal
  ½ cup firmly packed brown sugar
  1 tablespoon baking powder
  1 teaspoon cinnamon
  ½ teaspoon salt
1¼ cups milk
  ¼ cup oil
  ½ cup (1 medium) chopped, peeled apple
  1 egg, slightly beaten
  ¼ cup Sweet Pepper Jelly (see Index) or favorite jelly

Heat oven to 375°F. Grease 12 muffin cups or line with paper baking cups. Lightly spoon flour into measuring cup; level off. In large bowl, combine flour, cornmeal, brown sugar, baking powder, cinnamon and salt. Stir in milk, oil, apple and egg just until dry particles are moistened. Fill prepared muffin cups ½ full. Spoon 1 teaspoon jelly onto center of each muffin. Carefully spoon remaining batter evenly over jelly to cover. Bake at 375°F. for 20 to 22 minutes or until light golden brown. 12 muffins.

HIGH ALTITUDE—Above 3500 Feet: Increase flour to 2 cups plus 2 tablespoons.

For an elegant entertaining idea, combine Carrot Orange Soup and Broccoli Lemon Soup in the same bowl. Pour simultaneously from opposite sides of the bowl, then swirl with a table knife.

Broccoli Lemon Soup

2 cups chopped fresh broccoli
½ cup chopped onion
1 chicken-flavor bouillon cube or 1 teaspoon chicken-flavor instant bouillon
1½ cups water
½ teaspoon grated lemon peel
2 tablespoons margarine or butter
2 tablespoons flour
⅛ teaspoon salt
⅛ teaspoon white pepper
⅛ teaspoon nutmeg
1 cup milk

FOOD PROCESSOR DIRECTIONS: In medium saucepan, combine broccoli, onion, bouillon and water. Bring to a boil. Reduce heat; cover and simmer 11 minutes or until broccoli is tender. Pour ½ of mixture into food processor bowl with metal blade or blender container. Add lemon peel; puree until smooth. Repeat with remaining mixture. In same saucepan, melt margarine. Stir in flour, salt, white pepper and nutmeg; cook until mixture is smooth and bubbly. Gradually add milk. Cook until mixture boils and thickens, stirring constantly. Stir in broccoli mixture; heat thoroughly. 3 (1-cup) servings.

MICROWAVE DIRECTIONS: In 1½-quart microwave-safe casserole, combine broccoli, onion, bouillon and ½ **cup water**. Cover; microwave on HIGH for 5 to 7 minutes or until broccoli is tender, stirring once halfway through cooking. Add **1 cup** water. Puree broccoli mixture as directed above. In same microwave-safe casserole, microwave margarine on HIGH for 20 to 30 seconds or until melted. Stir in flour, salt, white pepper and nutmeg until smooth. Stir in milk, blending well. Microwave on HIGH for 4 to 5 minutes or until thickened, stirring every 2 minutes. Stir in pureed vegetables. Microwave on MEDIUM for 3 to 4 minutes or until thoroughly heated.

NUTRITION INFORMATION PER SERVING			
SERVING SIZE:		PERCENT U.S. RDA	
1 CUP		PER SERVING	
CALORIES	170	PROTEIN	8%
PROTEIN	6g	VITAMIN A	45%
CARBOHYDRATE	13g	VITAMIN C	70%
FAT	10g	THIAMINE	6%
CHOLESTEROL	6mg	RIBOFLAVIN	10%
SODIUM	550mg	NIACIN	4%
POTASSIUM	370mg	CALCIUM	15%
		IRON	4%

Pictured on previous page: Broccoli Lemon Soup and Carrot Orange Soup, swirled together

An easy, creamy soup with a delicate orange flavor. Add fun to your meal by serving with Broccoli Lemon Soup as described in that recipe's introduction.

Carrot Orange Soup

- 1 cup sliced carrots
- ½ cup chopped onion
- ½ teaspoon grated orange peel
- 1 chicken-flavor bouillon cube or 1 teaspoon chicken-flavor instant bouillon
- 1½ cups water
- 2 tablespoons margarine or butter
- 2 tablespoons flour
- ⅛ teaspoon salt
- ⅛ teaspoon white pepper
- ⅛ teaspoon nutmeg
- 1¼ cups milk

FOOD PROCESSOR DIRECTIONS: In medium saucepan, combine carrots, onion, orange peel, bouillon and water. Bring to a boil. Reduce heat; cover and simmer 14 minutes or until carrots are tender. Pour mixture into food processor bowl with metal blade or blender container; puree until smooth. In same saucepan, melt margarine. Stir in flour, salt, white pepper and nutmeg; cook until mixture is smooth and bubbly. Gradually add milk. Cook until mixture boils and thickens, stirring constantly. Stir in carrot mixture; heat thoroughly. 3 (1-cup) servings.

MICROWAVE DIRECTIONS: In 1½-quart microwave-safe casserole, combine carrots, onion, orange peel, bouillon and ½ **cup** water. Cover; microwave on HIGH for 8 to 10 minutes or until carrots are tender, stirring once halfway through cooking. Add **1 cup** water. Puree carrot mixture as directed above. In same microwave-safe casserole, microwave margarine on HIGH for 30 seconds or until melted. Stir in flour, salt, white pepper and nutmeg until smooth. Stir in milk, blending well. Microwave on HIGH for 4 to 5 minutes or until thickened, stirring every 2 minutes. Stir in pureed vegetables. Microwave on MEDIUM for 3 to 4 minutes or until thoroughly heated.

NUTRITION INFORMATION PER SERVING

SERVING SIZE: 1 CUP		PERCENT U.S. RDA PER SERVING	
CALORIES	170	PROTEIN	8%
PROTEIN	5g	VITAMIN A	240%
CARBOHYDRATE	16g	VITAMIN C	8%
FAT	10g	THIAMINE	8%
CHOLESTEROL	8mg	RIBOFLAVIN	10%
SODIUM	560mg	NIACIN	4%
POTASSIUM	350mg	CALCIUM	15%
		IRON	2%

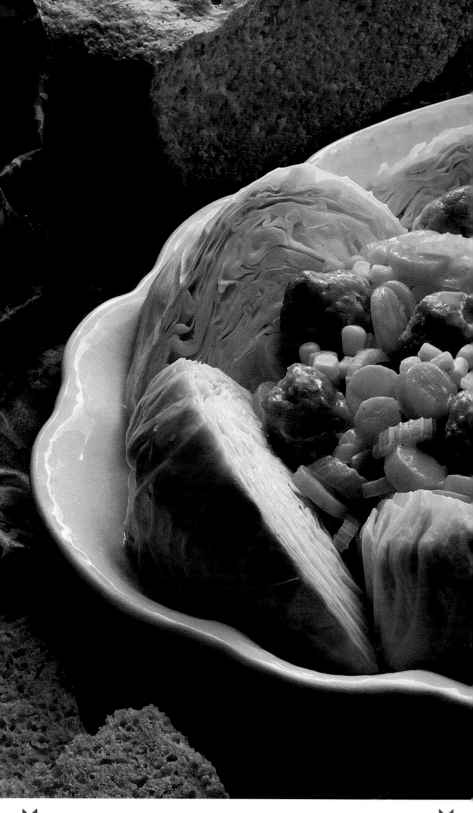

A colorful array of vegetables combine with pork sausage to create this robust stew. The steamed cabbage wedges arranged around the edge of the serving platter complement the stew.

Hearty Meatball and Vegetable Stew

        1 lb. bulk pork sausage
        2 tablespoons oil
      1/4 cup flour
      1/8 teaspoon pepper
        1 cup water
10 3/4-oz. can condensed chicken
           broth
        3 carrots, sliced
        2 stalks celery, sliced
        1 large (1 cup) onion, sliced
    12-oz. can Green Giant®
           Niblets® Whole Kernel
           Golden Sweet Corn,
           undrained
        2 cups water
        1 medium head cabbage, cut
           into 8 wedges

Shape pork sausage into 25 to 30 1-inch balls. In large skillet or Dutch oven, brown meatballs in oil, carefully turning to brown evenly. Remove meatballs from skillet. Reserve 2 tablespoons meat drippings in skillet; stir in flour and pepper. Gradually add 1 cup water and chicken broth. Cook until mixture boils and thickens, stirring constantly. Add carrots, celery, onion and meatballs. Simmer uncovered for 20 to 30 minutes or until vegetables are tender and stew is thickened, stirring occasionally. Add corn; heat thoroughly.

In large skillet or saucepan, heat 2 cups water to boiling; add cabbage. Cover and cook 8 minutes or until crisp-tender; drain. Arrange cabbage wedges in a ring, cut side down, around edge of serving platter; spoon stew into center of cabbage ring. 6 servings.

NUTRITION INFORMATION PER SERVING
SERVING SIZE: PERCENT U.S. RDA
1/6 OF RECIPE   PER SERVING

CALORIES	330	PROTEIN	20%
PROTEIN	14g	VITAMIN A	210%
CARBOHYDRATE	30g	VITAMIN C	100%
FAT	17g	THIAMINE	30%
CHOLESTEROL	30mg	RIBOFLAVIN	15%
SODIUM	960mg	NIACIN	20%
POTASSIUM	870mg	CALCIUM	10%
		IRON	10%

This is a quick and easy version of the classic New England chowder.

Potato Clam Chowder

        3 tablespoons margarine
           or butter
      1/2 cup chopped onion
      1/2 cup sliced celery
        2 carrots, thinly sliced
        2 cups water
        1 chicken-flavor bouillon
           cube or 1 teaspoon
           instant chicken
           bouillon
           Dash pepper
  2 (6 1/2-oz.) cans minced clams,
           undrained
     1 1/4 cups Hungry Jack®
           Mashed Potato Flakes
        1 cup milk

In large saucepan, melt margarine; stir in onion, celery and carrots. Cook over medium heat for 5 minutes, stirring occasionally. Add water, bouillon and pepper; stir until bouillon is dissolved. Bring to a boil; cover and simmer 15 minutes or until carrots are tender. Stir in clams, potato flakes and milk. Cook, stirring constantly, until throughly heated and smooth. 6 (1-cup) servings.

NUTRITION INFORMATION PER SERVING
SERVING SIZE: PERCENT U.S. RDA
1 CUP   PER SERVING

CALORIES	160	PROTEIN	10%
PROTEIN	8g	VITAMIN A	140%
CARBOHYDRATE	17g	VITAMIN C	8%
FAT	7g	THIAMINE	4%
CHOLESTEROL	25mg	RIBOFLAVIN	10%
SODIUM	630mg	NIACIN	6%
POTASSIUM	450mg	CALCIUM	10%
		IRON	15%

Pictured on previous page:
Hearty Meatball and Vegetable Stew

This recipe is a great party idea! Hot Roll Mix is used for an elegant presentation of two popular sandwich fillings.

Crisscross Sandwich Loaves

BREAD

16-oz. pkg. Pillsbury Hot Roll Mix
  1 tablespoon dry mustard
  1 cup hot tap water (110 to 120°F.)
  2 tablespoons margarine or butter, softened
  1 egg

FILLINGS

4-oz. pkg. thinly sliced ham
  8 oz. (8 slices) natural Swiss cheese
  ½ cup Quick Pickles (see Index) or sliced dill pickles, well drained
3-oz. pkg. thinly sliced corned beef
  8 oz. (1 cup) sauerkraut, squeezed to drain
  ¼ cup thousand island dressing

In large bowl, combine flour mixture with yeast from foil packet and mustard; mix well. Stir in hot water, margarine and egg until dough pulls away from sides of bowl. Turn dough out onto lightly floured surface. With greased or floured hands, shape dough into a ball. Knead dough for 5 minutes or until smooth. If necessary, sprinkle flour over surface to reduce stickiness. Cover dough with large bowl; let rest 5 minutes.

Grease large cookie sheet. Divide dough into two equal pieces. Roll one piece into 13x9-inch rectangle. Arrange ham lengthwise down center ⅓ of rectangle. Layer with half of cheese; top with pickles. Make cuts 1 inch apart on each side of rectangle just to edge of filling. Fold strips of dough at an angle across filling, overlapping ends and alternating from side to side. Pinch ends to seal. Place on one side of prepared cookie sheet. Roll second piece of dough to 13x9-inch rectangle. Arrange corned beef lengthwise down center ⅓ of rectangle; top with sauerkraut, dressing and remaining cheese. Shape as directed above. Place on same cookie sheet; cover completely with towel. Let dough rise 30 minutes on cookie sheet set over large pan to which hot water has been added. Heat oven to 375°F. Bake for 20 to 25 minutes or until golden brown. 8 servings.

HIGH ALTITUDE—Above 3500 Feet: No change.

NUTRITION INFORMATION PER SERVING

SERVING SIZE: 1/8 OF RECIPE		PERCENT U.S. RDA PER SERVING	
CALORIES	450	PROTEIN	35%
PROTEIN	21g	VITAMIN A	8%
CARBOHYDRATE	47g	VITAMIN C	6%
FAT	19g	THIAMINE	35%
CHOLESTEROL	80mg	RIBOFLAVIN	30%
SODIUM	1030mg	NIACIN	20%
POTASSIUM	220mg	CALCIUM	30%
		IRON	15%

Classically delicious!

Best Ever
Beer Cheese Soup

¼ cup margarine or butter
1 cup chopped onions
½ cup chopped celery
½ cup chopped carrot
¼ cup chopped fresh
    parsley
2 garlic cloves, crushed
¼ cup flour
3 teaspoons dry mustard
⅛ teaspoon pepper
2 cups half-and-half or
    milk
1 cup ⅓-less-salt chicken
    broth
12 oz. (2½ cups) cubed
    American process
    cheese
1 (12 oz.) can beer
2 cups popped popcorn

Melt margarine in large saucepan or
Dutch oven over medium heat. Stir in
onions, celery, carrot, parsley and
garlic. Cook over medium heat 5 to
6 minutes or until vegetables are crisp-
tender. Stir in flour, mustard and
pepper; mix well. Cook 1 minute,
stirring constantly. Gradually add half-
and-half and chicken broth; mix well.

Cook uncovered over medium heat
10 to 15 minutes or until soup is
thickened and thoroughly heated.
Stir in cheese and beer; cook
5 to 8 minutes or until cheese
is melted, stirring frequently. DO
NOT BOIL. Garnish with popcorn.
7 (1-cup) servings.

NUTRITION INFORMATION PER SERVING

SERVING SIZE: 1 CUP		PERCENT U.S. RDA PER SERVING	
CALORIES	410	PROTEIN	25%
PROTEIN	15g	VITAMIN A	70%
CARBOHYDRATE	15g	VITAMIN C	6%
FAT	30g	THIAMINE	8%
CHOLESTEROL	71mg	RIBOFLAVIN	20%
SODIUM	940mg	NIACIN	4%
POTASSIUM	320mg	CALCIUM	40%
		IRON	4%

*Savory and hearty, this recipe is the
perfect way to use the turkey leftovers.*

Turkey Noodle Soup

Bones and trimmings from 9 to
    15-lb. turkey
3 quarts water
2 teaspoons salt
¼ teaspoon poultry seasoning
3 chicken-flavor bouillon cubes or
    3 teaspoons chicken-flavor
    instant bouillon cubes
1 bay leaf
½ cup chopped celery
½ cup finely chopped onion
3 carrots, sliced
2 cups fine egg noodles

Break up turkey to fit 5-quart Dutch
oven. Add water, salt, poultry
seasoning, bouillon cubes and bay leaf.
Bring to a boil. Reduce heat to low;
cover and cook 1 hour. Remove bones
from broth; strain broth, if desired.
When cool enough to handle, cut any
meat from the bones; return meat to
broth. Add celery, onion and carrots.
Cover; cook over low heat 15 minutes.
Add noodles; cook uncovered
15 minutes or until noodles are tender,
stirring occasionally. Remove bay leaf.
Season to taste with salt and pepper, if
desired. 10 (1½-cup) servings.

NUTRITION INFORMATION PER SERVING

SERVING SIZE: 1-1/2 CUPS		PERCENT U.S. RDA PER SERVING	
CALORIES	130	PROTEIN	20%
PROTEIN	14g	VITAMIN A	120%
CARBOHYDRATE	11g	VITAMIN C	2%
FAT	3g	THIAMINE	10%
CHOLESTEROL	43mg	RIBOFLAVIN	8%
SODIUM	820mg	NIACIN	15%
POTASSIUM	260mg	CALCIUM	2%
		IRON	8%

Slices of Polish sausage add flavor to this old-fashioned recipe.

Cabbage Soup with Sausage

  3 Polish sausages, cut into
    ½-inch pieces
  1 small head cabbage, coarsely
    chopped
  1 medium onion, sliced
  4 carrots, thinly sliced
2½ quarts chicken broth
  ¼ teaspoon pepper

In Dutch oven or saucepan, brown sliced sausages; drain, reserving 2 tablespoons drippings. Set sausages aside. Add cabbage and onion to drippings; cook over medium heat until lightly browned, about 7 minutes. Add carrots and chicken broth. Cover; simmer about 1 hour or until vegetables are tender. Add pepper and sausages; heat thoroughly. 9 (1½-cup) servings.

NUTRITION INFORMATION PER SERVING
SERVING SIZE: PERCENT U.S. RDA
1-1/2 CUPS   PER SERVING
CALORIES   150   PROTEIN   15%
PROTEIN   10g   VITAMIN A   180%
CARBOHYDRATE   7g   VITAMIN C   20%
FAT   9g   THIAMINE   10%
CHOLESTEROL   20mg   RIBOFLAVIN   8%
SODIUM   1100mg   NIACIN   25%
POTASSIUM   490mg   CALCIUM   4%
                        IRON   6%

Enjoy the wonderful aroma of an old-fashioned country kitchen as you bake this easy-to-prepare yeast bread from Hot Roll Mix.

Hot Roll Wheat Batter Bread

16-oz. pkg. Pillsbury Hot Roll Mix
  ½ cup wheat germ
1¼ cups hot tap water (110 to
     120°F.)
  2 tablespoons molasses
  2 tablespoons oil
  1 egg

In large bowl, combine flour mixture with yeast from foil packet and wheat germ; mix well. Stir in hot water, molasses, oil and egg until well mixed (batter will be sticky). Cover; let dough rise in bowl 30 minutes, or until light and doubled in size, on wire rack set over large pan to which hot water has been added.

Grease 2-quart casserole. Stir down dough; spread in prepared casserole. Cover; let rise over hot water 30 minutes or until light and doubled in size.

Heat oven to 375°F. Bake 30 to 35 minutes or until deep golden brown. Immediately remove from casserole. 1 (16-slice) loaf.

HIGH ALTITUDE—Above 3500 Feet: No change.

NUTRITION INFORMATION PER SERVING
SERVING SIZE: PERCENT U.S. RDA
1 SLICE   PER SERVING
CALORIES   140   PROTEIN   6%
PROTEIN   4g   VITAMIN A   *
CARBOHYDRATE   24g   VITAMIN C   *
FAT   3g   THIAMINE   15%
CHOLESTEROL   15mg   RIBOFLAVIN   10%
SODIUM   200mg   NIACIN   8%
POTASSIUM   95mg   CALCIUM   *
                        IRON   8%
*Contains less than 2% of the U.S. RDA of this nutrient.

We've added apple and a hint of orange to traditional French onion soup for a new taste sensation. It's topped off with a toasted, flavorful French bread slice.

Apple Onion Soup with Toasted Cheese Croutons

SOUP

3 tablespoons margarine or butter
8 cups (2 large) halved and sliced white onions
3 cups water
1 cup apple juice
½ cup white wine
½ teaspoon grated orange peel
2 (10½-oz.) cans condensed beef broth
1 medium apple, peeled and grated

CROUTONS

¼ cup margarine or butter, softened
2 tablespoons grated Parmesan cheese
2 tablespoons finely chopped parsley
1 garlic clove, minced
6 (1-inch thick) slices French bread

In Dutch oven, saute onions in 3 tablespoons margarine 10 minutes or until tender. Add remaining soup ingredients. Bring to a boil. Reduce heat; cover and simmer 30 minutes.

Heat oven to 350°F. In small bowl, combine ¼ cup margarine, Parmesan cheese, parsley and garlic. Spread on one side of French bread slices; place on ungreased cookie sheet. Bake at 350°F. for 8 minutes or until lightly browned. Garnish each serving with 1 crouton. 6 (1 ½-cup) servings.

NUTRITION INFORMATION PER SERVING			
SERVING SIZE: 1/6 OF RECIPE		PERCENT U.S. RDA PER SERVING	
CALORIES	320	PROTEIN	15%
PROTEIN	9g	VITAMIN A	10%
CARBOHYDRATE	34g	VITAMIN C	10%
FAT	15g	THIAMINE	10%
CHOLESTEROL	2mg	RIBOFLAVIN	8%
SODIUM	920mg	NIACIN	8%
POTASSIUM	330mg	CALCIUM	8%
		IRON	10%

Like Boston brown bread, molasses sweetens and flavors this moist roll. Enjoy them warm with plenty of butter alongside a bowl of Frankfurter Lentil Soup (see Index).

Brown Bread Gems

1½ cups Pillsbury's BEST® Whole Wheat Flour
½ cup yellow cornmeal
½ cup chopped dates
⅓ cup sugar
¼ cup chopped nuts
1 teaspoon baking soda
½ teaspoon salt
1 cup buttermilk*
¼ cup molasses

Heat oven to 375°F. Grease bottoms only of 12 muffin cups. Lightly spoon flour into measuring cup; level off. In medium bowl, combine flour, cornmeal, dates, sugar, nuts, baking soda and salt; blend well. Add buttermilk and molasses; stir just until dry ingredients are moistened. Fill prepared muffin cups about ¾ full. Bake at 375°F. for 16 to 25 minutes or until toothpick inserted in center comes out clean. Cool 1 minute before removing from pan. Serve warm. 12 muffins.

TIP: *To substitute for buttermilk, use 1 tablespoon vinegar or lemon juice plus milk to make 1 cup.

HIGH ALTITUDE—Above 3500 Feet: No change.

NUTRITION INFORMATION PER SERVING			
SERVING SIZE: 1 MUFFIN		PERCENT U.S. RDA PER SERVING	
CALORIES	160	PROTEIN	6%
PROTEIN	4g	VITAMIN A	*
CARBOHYDRATE	31g	VITAMIN C	*
FAT	2g	THIAMINE	8%
CHOLESTEROL	0mg	RIBOFLAVIN	4%
SODIUM	210mg	NIACIN	4%
POTASSIUM	230mg	CALCIUM	6%
		IRON	6%

*Contains less than 2% of the U.S. RDA of this nutrient.

Apple Onion Soup with Toasted Cheese Croutons

Potato flakes simplify the preparation of these unleavened potato cakes. They are a Scandinavian specialty served as an alternative to bread.

Hungry Jack® Lefse

3 cups Hungry Jack® Mashed Potato Flakes
1 cup water
2 tablespoons margarine or butter
2 teaspoons salt
1 cup milk
¾ to 1 cup Pillsbury's BEST® All Purpose or Unbleached Flour

Heat electric lefse griddle or electric skillet to highest temperature setting. DO NOT GREASE GRIDDLE OR SKILLET. Measure potato flakes into large bowl. In small saucepan, heat water, margarine and salt to rolling boil. Remove from heat; add milk. Add liquid all at once to potato flakes, stirring until all flakes are moistened (mixture will be crumbly). Gradually add flour to potato mixture, working with hands until a soft dough forms and is of rolling consistency. (Avoid adding too much flour.) Form dough into a roll 10 inches long and about 2 inches in diameter. Cut roll into ½-inch slices. Cover with plastic wrap while rolling out each lefse.

On well-floured pastry cloth, roll out one slice of dough until paper-thin.* Transfer to heated griddle using lefse stick or long spatula. Bake until brown spots appear on bottom surface, about 1 minute. Turn and bake other side, about 30 to 45 seconds. Place baked lefse between cloth towels to prevent lefse from drying. Repeat with remaining slices. Cool completely. To serve, spread with butter; fold into quarters.** 20 lefse.

TIPS: *For best results, use rolling pin covered with pastry stocking. Flour rolling pin and pastry cloth before rolling out each lefse.
  **For smaller servings, cut in half or into wedges and roll up. Sprinkle with sugar, if desired.

NUTRITION INFORMATION PER SERVING
SERVING SIZE: PERCENT U.S. RDA
1 LEFSE   PER SERVING

CALORIES	70	PROTEIN	2%
PROTEIN	2g	VITAMIN A	*
CARBOHYDRATE	12g	VITAMIN C	2%
FAT	2g	THIAMINE	4%
CHOLESTEROL	0mg	RIBOFLAVIN	4%
SODIUM	240mg	NIACIN	2%
POTASSIUM	150mg	CALCIUM	2%
		IRON	2%

*Contains less than 2% of the U.S. RDA of this nutrient.

Extended-Use Recipe

Nutritious and full of flavor, these sandwiches are a great way to use up leftover pot roast.

Zippy Sprout 'n Beef Pockets

8-oz. carton (1 cup) plain yogurt
½ teaspoon dry mustard
2 teaspoons prepared horseradish
2 (6-inch) pocket breads
8 oz. sliced, cooked roast beef
1 cup alfalfa sprouts
1 small tomato, sliced

In small bowl, combine yogurt, mustard and horseradish; blend well. Cut pocket breads in half. Spoon 2 tablespoons of the yogurt mixture into each pocket bread half; fill each with ¼ of the beef, sprouts and tomato. Serve with remaining yogurt mixture. 4 sandwiches.

NUTRITION INFORMATION PER SERVING
SERVING SIZE: PERCENT U.S. RDA
1 SANDWICH   PER SERVING

CALORIES	280	PROTEIN	40%
PROTEIN	25g	VITAMIN A	6%
CARBOHYDRATE	28g	VITAMIN C	10%
FAT	8g	THIAMINE	15%
CHOLESTEROL	60mg	RIBOFLAVIN	20%
SODIUM	85mg	NIACIN	20%
POTASSIUM	390mg	CALCIUM	15%
		IRON	20%

Frankfurters add a new taste to this thick and hearty country-style soup. For a more traditional flavor, use leftover ham.

Frankfurter Lentil Soup

16-oz. pkg. (about 2½ cups) dry lentils
9 cups water
½ cup chopped onion
½ cup thinly sliced carrot
½ cup chopped celery
1 teaspoon salt
½ teaspoon oregano
⅛ teaspoon cayenne
1 garlic clove, minced
¼ cup red wine vinegar
6-oz. can tomato paste
6 frankfurters, sliced, or 1½ cups cubed, cooked ham
1 medium red or green bell pepper, chopped

Wash and sort lentils. In Dutch oven, combine lentils, water, onion, carrot, celery, salt, oregano, cayenne and garlic. Bring to a boil. Reduce heat; cover and simmer 1 hour or until lentils are soft. Stir in wine vinegar, tomato paste, frankfurters and red pepper. Simmer covered an additional 30 minutes, stirring occasionally. 9 (1½-cup) servings.

NUTRITION INFORMATION PER SERVING
SERVING SIZE: 1 1/2 CUPS

		PERCENT U.S. RDA PER SERVING	
CALORIES	320	PROTEIN	25%
PROTEIN	18g	VITAMIN A	60%
CARBOHYDRATE	38g	VITAMIN C	50%
FAT	12g	THIAMINE	15%
CHOLESTEROL	20mg	RIBOFLAVIN	10%
SODIUM	800mg	NIACIN	15%
POTASSIUM	720mg	CALCIUM	4%
		IRON	25%

Spark up a meal with this Mexican variation of grilled cheese sandwiches.

Grilled Chicken and Cheese

½ ripe avocado, peeled
4-oz. can diced green chiles, drained
8 slices Hot Roll Wheat Batter Bread (see Index) or whole wheat bread
2 boneless, skinless, cooked whole chicken breasts, thinly sliced, or 8 oz. thinly sliced cooked turkey
4 oz. (4 slices) Monterey jack cheese
1 medium tomato, thinly sliced
Margarine or butter, softened
Salsa, if desired

In small bowl, mash avocado; stir in green chiles.

To assemble sandwiches, spread 4 slices of bread evenly with avocado mixture. Top each with ¼ of chicken, cheese and tomato. Cover with remaining bread slices. Spread margarine on outsides of sandwiches; cut in half. Grill sandwiches on both sides over medium heat until bread begins to brown and cheese begins to melt. To serve, dip sandwiches in salsa. 4 sandwiches.

NUTRITION INFORMATION PER SERVING
SERVING SIZE: 1 SANDWICH

		PERCENT U.S. RDA PER SERVING	
CALORIES	680	PROTEIN	60%
PROTEIN	41g	VITAMIN A	80%
CARBOHYDRATE	55g	VITAMIN C	25%
FAT	33g	THIAMINE	40%
CHOLESTEROL	130mg	RIBOFLAVIN	40%
SODIUM	1230mg	NIACIN	80%
POTASSIUM	750mg	CALCIUM	30%
		IRON	25%

 COUNTRY COOKING

Side Dishes, Relishes & Preserves

Side Dishes, Relishes & Preserves

To serve now or preserve for later.

Garden goodness can extend well into fall, giving cooks glorious fruits and vegetables to enliven harvest menus. Squashes, cucumbers, pumpkins, potatoes, Brussels sprouts, red and green peppers and other hardy favorites continue to thrive despite falling temperatures. This chapter contains fresh approaches to serving this produce in its prime and for preserving those tastes well beyond the first frost.

The increasingly popular microwave oven plays a starring role. We have developed a marvelous array of microwave relishes and preserves—not at all difficult or time-consuming to prepare. With little equipment and few ingredients, you can produce creamy **Microwave Apple Butter,** zesty **Microwave Peach Chutney,** tangy **Sweet Pepper Jelly** and other jewel-tone gems to pass proudly at your table or give as colorful, tempting gifts. These microwave-prepared jam, jelly and relish recipes, particularly suited to today's smaller families, store in the refrigerator for peak-of-freshness flavors. Many of these creative combinations are unavailable in supermarkets, making them all the more interesting to serve as sparkling accompaniments to almost any entree.

The salads, **Spinach Timbales, Onion 'n Chive Mashed Potatoes** and other Americana adaptations are perfect for family dining and cooler weather entertaining. The origin of many of these recipes dates back to rural America where kitchen windows overlooked the family vegetable garden. Wonderful diversity comes from each cook's heritage; imaginative touches come from every cook's desire to add personal flourishes. Ideas abound in choice, blue-ribbon recipes like these to enhance each mealtime.

Pictured on previous page, left to right: Quick Straw-berry Jam p. 57 on Bacon Biscuit Wedges p. 38 and Pineapple Kiwifruit Jam p. 57

Excellent! Our taste panel gave this a four-star rating on taste and appearance.

Pineapple Kiwifruit Jam

4 kiwifruit, peeled, sliced
   ⅛-inch thick
3 cups sugar
¼ cup lime juice
8-oz. can crushed pineapple,
   undrained
3-oz. pkg. liquid fruit pectin
3 drops green food color

 MICROWAVE DIRECTIONS:
In 2-quart microwave-safe bowl,
combine kiwifruit, sugar, lime juice
and pineapple. Microwave on HIGH
for 11½ to 16 minutes or until mixture
comes to full rolling boil, stirring
every 2 minutes. Stir in liquid pectin.
Microwave on HIGH for 2 to
3 minutes or until mixture comes to
full rolling boil; continue to boil for
1 minute. Skim foam; stir in
food color.

Spoon into 5 clean, hot 8-oz. jars;
screw lids on firmly. Cool several
hours. Store in refrigerator up to
3 weeks or in freezer up to 3 months.
4½ cups.

NUTRITION INFORMATION PER SERVING			
SERVING SIZE:		PERCENT U.S. RDA	
1 TABLESPOON		PER SERVING	
CALORIES	35	PROTEIN	*
PROTEIN	0g	VITAMIN A	*
CARBOHYDRATE	10g	VITAMIN C	4%
FAT	0g	THIAMINE	*
CHOLESTEROL	0mg	RIBOFLAVIN	*
SODIUM	0mg	NIACIN	*
POTASSIUM	20mg	CALCIUM	*
		IRON	*

*Contains less than 2% of the U.S. RDA of this nutrient.

This beautiful, sparkling red jam can be made ahead to freeze for the holidays.

Quick Strawberry Jam

2 (10-oz.) pkg. frozen strawberries,
   thawed
¼ cup powdered fruit
   pectin
2 cups sugar
¼ teaspoon nutmeg
1 tablespoon lemon juice

MICROWAVE DIRECTIONS:
In 2-quart microwave-safe bowl,
combine strawberries and powdered
pectin; mix well. Microwave on
HIGH for 8 to 10 minutes or until
mixture comes to full rolling boil,
stirring every 2 minutes. Stir in sugar,
nutmeg and lemon juice. Microwave
on HIGH for 4 to 6 minutes or until
mixture comes to full rolling boil,
stirring once halfway through
cooking. Continue to boil for
1 minute. Skim foam.

Spoon into 4 clean, hot 8-oz. jars;
screw lids on firmly. Cool several
hours. Store in refrigerator up to
3 weeks or in freezer up to 3 months.
4 cups.

NUTRITION INFORMATION PER SERVING			
SERVING SIZE:		PERCENT U.S. RDA	
1 TABLESPOON		PER SERVING	
CALORIES	35	PROTEIN	*
PROTEIN	0g	VITAMIN A	*
CARBOHYDRATE	9g	VITAMIN C	6%
FAT	0g	THIAMINE	*
CHOLESTEROL	0mg	RIBOFLAVIN	*
SODIUM	0mg	NIACIN	*
POTASSIUM	10mg	CALCIUM	*
		IRON	*

*Contains less than 2% of the U.S. RDA of this nutrient.

Spread this zesty jelly and cream cheese on crackers for a tasty, quick appetizer, or make Apple Corn Muffins with Pepper Jelly (see Index) for a new taste treat. It also goes well with meats.

Sweet Pepper Jelly

NUTRITION INFORMATION PER SERVING

SERVING SIZE:		PERCENT U.S. RDA	
1 TABLESPOON		PER SERVING	
CALORIES	45	PROTEIN	*
PROTEIN	0g	VITAMIN A	*
CARBOHYDRATE	12g	VITAMIN C	20%
FAT	0g	THIAMINE	*
CHOLESTEROL	0mg	RIBOFLAVIN	*
SODIUM	10mg	NIACIN	*
POTASSIUM	30mg	CALCIUM	*
		IRON	*

*Contains less than 2% of the U.S. RDA of this nutrient.

4 cups (4 medium) green
   peppers, cut into 1-inch
   pieces
¾ cup cider vinegar
¾ cup apple juice
   Cold water
3 tablespoons powdered fruit
   pectin
¼ teaspoon salt
2½ cups sugar
3 drops green food color

FOOD PROCESSOR AND MICROWAVE DIRECTIONS: In food processor bowl with metal blade or blender container, puree peppers in vinegar. In 2-quart microwave-safe bowl, combine pepper mixture and apple juice. Microwave on HIGH for 10 to 12 minutes or until mixture comes to full rolling boil. Continue to boil for 7 minutes. Line colander with 2 layers of damp cheesecloth. Strain pepper liquid into bowl, allowing mixture to drain slowly; discard pulp. (A cloudy jelly will result if liquid is forced through colander.) Measure liquid; add water to total 2 cups. In clean 2-quart microwave-safe bowl, combine pepper liquid, powdered pectin and salt; mix well. Microwave on HIGH for 5 to 11 minutes or until mixture boils. Stir in sugar. Microwave on HIGH for 6 to 6½ minutes or until mixture comes to full rolling boil, stirring once halfway through cooking. Continue to boil for 1 minute. Skim foam; stir in food color.

Pour into 3 clean, hot 8-oz. jars; screw lids on firmly. Cool several hours. Store in refrigerator up to 3 weeks or in freezer up to 3 months. 3 cups.

The secret to these crunchy pickles is the standing time on ice. Using the microwave, you can prepare crispy, colorful refrigerator pickles in no time at all.

Quick Pickles

3 cups unpeeled and thinly sliced
   cucumbers
1 medium onion, sliced
1 small green bell pepper, cut into
   strips
1 small red bell pepper, cut into
   strips
1 small carrot, thinly sliced
1 garlic clove, crushed
1 teaspoon salt
8 cups ice cubes
¾ cup sugar
1 teaspoon mustard seed
¼ teaspoon celery seed
⅛ teaspoon tumeric
½ cup white vinegar

MICROWAVE DIRECTIONS: In large bowl, combine cucumbers, onion, peppers, carrot, garlic and salt. Add ice cubes and mix thoroughly. Let stand 3 hours. Using colander, drain well.

In 4-cup microwave-safe glass measuring cup, combine remaining ingredients. Microwave on HIGH for 2 to 5 minutes or until mixture boils; stir to dissolve sugar. In 1-quart jar, pack drained vegetables. Pour hot vinegar mixture over vegetables; cover. Let stand in refrigerator 24 hours before serving. Store in refrigerator. 4 cups.

NUTRITION INFORMATION: Variables in this recipe make it impossible to calculate nutrition information.

This relish is slightly tart and a nice change of pace.

Cranapple Raisin Relish

1 cup sugar
½ cup golden raisins
⅔ cup apple juice
¼ cup cider vinegar
1 teaspoon grated orange peel
½ teaspoon ginger
12-oz. pkg. (3 cups) fresh or frozen cranberries
1 medium apple, chopped
¼ cup coarsely chopped walnuts

▣ MICROWAVE DIRECTIONS: In 2-quart microwave-safe bowl, combine sugar, raisins, apple juice and vinegar. Cover with microwave-safe plastic wrap. Microwave on HIGH for 5 to 6 minutes or until mixture boils. Stir in orange peel, ginger, cranberries and apple. Cover; microwave on HIGH for 6 to 8 minutes or until cranberries pop, stirring once halfway through cooking time. Continue to microwave on HIGH for 1 minute or until slightly thickened. Stir in walnuts. Cover; store in refrigerator up to 2 weeks. 4 cups.

NUTRITION INFORMATION PER SERVING
SERVING SIZE: 1 TABLESPOON

		PERCENT U.S. RDA PER SERVING	
CALORIES	25	PROTEIN	*
PROTEIN	0g	VITAMIN A	*
CARBOHYDRATE	5g	VITAMIN C	*
FAT	0g	THIAMINE	*
CHOLESTEROL	0mg	RIBOFLAVIN	*
SODIUM	0mg	NIACIN	*
POTASSIUM	20mg	CALCIUM	*
		IRON	*

*Contains less than 2% of the U.S. RDA of this nutrient.

Try this quick and easy preparation of an old favorite.

Microwave Apple Butter

8 cups (9 medium) cored, quartered, peeled apples
2 cups apple cider or apple juice
1½ cups sugar
¾ teaspoon cinnamon
¼ teaspoon cloves
¼ teaspoon allspice

▣ ▣ FOOD PROCESSOR AND MICROWAVE DIRECTIONS: In 3-quart microwave-safe casserole, combine apples and cider. Microwave on HIGH for 12 to 15 minutes or until apples are tender, stirring twice during cooking. In food processor bowl with metal blade or blender container, process apple mixture until smooth. Return to casserole. Add sugar, cinnamon, cloves and allspice; blend well. Microwave on HIGH for 25 to 35 minutes or until thickened and dark brown, stirring once halfway through cooking. (Mixture will thicken as it cools.) Spoon into 4 clean, hot 8-oz. jars; screw lids on tightly. Store in refrigerator up to 3 weeks or in freezer up to 3 months. 4 cups.

NUTRITION INFORMATION PER SERVING
SERVING SIZE: 1 TABLESPOON

		PERCENT U.S. RDA PER SERVING	
CALORIES	30	PROTEIN	*
PROTEIN	0g	VITAMIN A	*
CARBOHYDRATE	8g	VITAMIN C	*
FAT	0g	THIAMINE	*
CHOLESTEROL	0mg	RIBOFLAVIN	*
SODIUM	0mg	NIACIN	*
POTASSIUM	30mg	CALCIUM	*
		IRON	*

*Contains less than 2% of the U.S. RDA of this nutrient.

 SIDE DISHES, RELISHES & PRESERVES

Add snap to an everyday meal with these colorful mouth-puckering pickles.

Pickled Peppers

1 tablespoon sugar
1 tablespoon salt
2 cups water
1 cup white vinegar
1 red bell pepper, cut into sixths
1 yellow bell pepper, cut into sixths
1 green bell pepper, cut into sixths
2 garlic cloves, halved
1 small onion, sliced and separated
    into rings
1 sprig fresh tarragon or
    ¼ teaspoon dried tarragon

MICROWAVE DIRECTIONS:
In 2-quart microwave-safe bowl, combine sugar, salt, water and vinegar. Microwave on HIGH for 8 to 14 minutes or until mixture boils. In 1-quart jar, pack remaining ingredients. Pour hot vinegar mixture over vegetables; cover. Let stand in refrigerator 1 week before serving. Store in refrigerator. 1 quart.

NUTRITION INFORMATION: Variables in this recipe make it impossible to calculate nutrition information.

Orange, tangerine and lemon team up for an exceptional marmalade prepared in the microwave.

Citrus Marmalade

1 medium orange
1 medium tangerine
1 medium lemon
1½ cups water
⅛ teaspoon baking soda
3 cups sugar
3-oz. pkg. liquid fruit pectin

MICROWAVE DIRECTIONS:
Score outer peel of fruit into quarters. Remove thin layer of peel a quarter at a time. Discard white membrane from peel and fruit. Cut peel into very thin strips. In 2-quart microwave-safe bowl, combine peel, water and soda. Cover; microwave on HIGH for 5 to 8 minutes or until mixture comes to a full rolling boil; continue to boil for 10 minutes, stirring once halfway through cooking.

Meanwhile, in shallow bowl, finely chop fruit, being careful not to lose any juice. Add fruit with juice to peel mixture. Cover; microwave on HIGH for 3 to 4 minutes or until mixture comes to full rolling boil; continue to boil for 10 minutes, stirring once halfway through cooking. Stir sugar and pectin into 2 cups of fruit mixture; discard excess mixture. Microwave on HIGH for 6½ to 9 minutes or until mixture comes to full rolling boil, stirring twice during cooking. Continue to boil for 1 minute.

Spoon into 3 clean, hot 8-oz. jars; screw lids on firmly. Cool several hours. Store in refrigerator up to 3 weeks or in freezer up to 3 months. 3 cups.

NUTRITION INFORMATION:
Variables in this recipe make it impossible to calculate nutrition information.

Chutney is a condiment of East Indian origin. Serve it as an accompaniment to ham or pork.

Microwave Peach Chutney

⅓ cup firmly packed brown sugar
⅓ cup raisins
¼ cup chopped onion
2 tablespoons cornstarch
1 tablespoon chopped crystallized ginger
⅛ teaspoon allspice
⅛ teaspoon cayenne pepper
½ cup cider vinegar
⅓ cup honey
29-oz. can peach halves, drained, finely chopped

MICROWAVE DIRECTIONS:
In 2-quart microwave-safe bowl, combine all ingredients. Microwave on HIGH for 9 to 14 minutes or until mixture boils and thickens, stirring every 2 minutes.

Spoon into 3 clean, hot 8-oz. jars; screw lids on firmly. Store in refrigerator up to 3 weeks. 3 cups.

NUTRITION INFORMATION PER SERVING			
SERVING SIZE: 1 TABLESPOON		PERCENT U.S. RDA PER SERVING	
CALORIES	25	PROTEIN	*
PROTEIN	0g	VITAMIN A	*
CARBOHYDRATE	6g	VITAMIN C	*
FAT	0g	THIAMINE	*
CHOLESTEROL	0mg	RIBOFLAVIN	*
SODIUM	0mg	NIACIN	*
POTASSIUM	45mg	CALCIUM	*
		IRON	*

*Contains less than 2% of the U.S. RDA of this nutrient.

If you like apple butter, you'll love pumpkin butter! Try it on muffins, quick breads or toasted raisin bread.

Pumpkin Butter

16-oz. can (2 cups) pumpkin
3 tablespoons powdered fruit pectin
1 teaspoon cinnamon
½ teaspoon allspice
2¼ cups sugar

MICROWAVE DIRECTIONS:
In 2-quart microwave-safe bowl, combine pumpkin, powdered pectin, cinnamon and allspice; mix well. Microwave on HIGH for 6 minutes or until mixture is very hot, stirring every 2 minutes. Add sugar; mix well. Microwave on HIGH for 5 to 10 minutes or until mixture comes to full rolling boil, stirring once during cooking. Continue to boil for 1 minute.

Spoon into 3 clean, hot 8-oz. jars; screw lids on firmly. Cool several hours. Store in refrigerator up to 3 weeks or in freezer up to 3 months. 3 cups.

NUTRITION INFORMATION PER SERVING

SERVING SIZE: 1 TABLESPOON		PERCENT U.S. RDA PER SERVING	
CALORIES	40	PROTEIN	*
PROTEIN	0g	VITAMIN A	40%
CARBOHYDRATE	11g	VITAMIN C	*
FAT	0g	THIAMINE	*
CHOLESTEROL	0mg	RIBOFLAVIN	*
SODIUM	0mg	NIACIN	*
POTASSIUM	20mg	CALCIUM	*
		IRON	*

*Contains less than 2% of the U.S. RDA of this nutrient.

The fragrant citrus and spice aroma of fruit soup as it cooks reminds me of the holidays at Grandma's house. This classic Scandinavian soup, made with dried fruit, has been passed down through generations. It gained popularity at a time when fresh fruit was an expensive luxury during winter months. It is served as dessert or a meal accompaniment.

Scandinavian Fruit Soup

- ½ cup sugar
- 4 cups water
- ¼ cup quick cooking tapioca
- ½ cup raisins
- 8-oz. pkg. (2 cups) mixed dried fruit
- ½ lemon, finely chopped (including peel)
- 1 stick cinnamon

In large saucepan, combine sugar and water. Bring to a boil. Gradually add tapioca, stirring constantly. Add remaining ingredients; cover and simmer 1½ hours, stirring occasionally. Discard cinnamon stick. Serve hot. 10 (½-cup) servings.

NUTRITION INFORMATION PER SERVING

SERVING SIZE: 1/2 CUP		PERCENT U.S. RDA PER SERVING	
CALORIES	130	PROTEIN	*
PROTEIN	1g	VITAMIN A	6%
CARBOHYDRATE	32g	VITAMIN C	4%
FAT	0g	THIAMINE	*
CHOLESTEROL	0mg	RIBOFLAVIN	*
SODIUM	5mg	NIACIN	*
POTASSIUM	250mg	CALCIUM	*
		IRON	2%

*Contains less than 2% of the U.S. RDA of this nutrient.

This colorful gelatin salad is a refreshing accompaniment to a holiday meal.

Cranberry Apple Grape Molded Salad

- 2 cups cranberry juice
- 6-oz. pkg. raspberry flavor gelatin
- ½ cup port wine
- ½ cup water
- 1 cup seedless green grapes
- 2 cups diced apples
- ½ cup chopped nuts

In large saucepan, heat cranberry juice to boiling; stir in gelatin until dissolved. Stir in wine and water. Arrange grapes in bottom of ungreased 6½-cup mold. Pour small amount of gelatin over grapes, being careful not to totally cover grapes; chill. Chill remaining gelatin until mixture begins to thicken but not set; fold in apples and nuts. Pour over grape layer in mold. Chill until firm. Unmold onto serving plate. 10 (½-cup) servings.

NUTRITION INFORMATION PER SERVING

SERVING SIZE: 1/2 CUP		PERCENT U.S. RDA PER SERVING	
CALORIES	170	PROTEIN	4%
PROTEIN	3g	VITAMIN A	*
CARBOHYDRATE	30g	VITAMIN C	15%
FAT	4g	THIAMINE	2%
CHOLESTEROL	0mg	RIBOFLAVIN	*
SODIUM	60mg	NIACIN	*
POTASSIUM	140mg	CALCIUM	*
		IRON	2%

*Contains less than 2% of the U.S. RDA of this nutrient.

Here's a deliciously different way to prepare squash. It is an especially tasty accompaniment to pork chops or poultry.

Harvest Time Squash

1 medium (1¼ lb.) acorn squash, halved, seeded
3 cups Green Giant® American Mixtures® San Francisco Style Frozen Broccoli, Carrots, Water Chestnuts and Red Peppers
1 tablespoon margarine or butter, melted
Salt
Pepper
2 oz. (½ cup) shredded American cheese

Heat oven to 400°F. Arrange squash halves cut side down in ungreased 13x9-inch pan. Bake at 400°F. for 30 minutes or until squash is tender.

Meanwhile, cook vegetables as directed on package. Turn squash cut side up. Pour margarine into cavities; sprinkle with salt and pepper. Spoon vegetables into cavities; sprinkle with cheese. Return to oven; bake an additional 3 to 5 minutes or until cheese is melted. Cut each stuffed squash in half. 4 servings.

■ MICROWAVE DIRECTIONS: Arrange squash halves cut side down in ungreased shallow microwave-safe dish. Cover with microwave-safe plastic wrap. Microwave on HIGH for 7 to 9 minutes or until squash is tender; set aside. Cook vegetables in microwave as directed on package. Stuff squash as directed above; return to microwave-safe dish. Microwave on HIGH for 1½ to 2 minutes or until cheese is melted. Cut each stuffed squash in half.

NUTRITION INFORMATION PER SERVING
SERVING SIZE: PERCENT U.S. RDA
1/4 OF RECIPE PER SERVING

CALORIES	220	PROTEIN	15%
PROTEIN	9g	VITAMIN A	100%
CARBOHYDRATE	20g	VITAMIN C	90%
FAT	12g	THIAMINE	15%
CHOLESTEROL	25mg	RIBOFLAVIN	10%
SODIUM	740mg	NIACIN	6%
POTASSIUM	680mg	CALCIUM	25%
		IRON	8%

This recipe is a snap to prepare with canned fruits, and it's elegant enough for company. The curry and honey taste sensational with the fruit.

Curried Fruit Bake

20-oz. can pineapple chunks, well drained
16-oz. can pear halves, well drained
16-oz. can dark sweet cherries, well drained
17-oz. can apricot halves, well drained
⅓ cup margarine or butter
⅓ cup honey
2 teaspoons curry powder

Heat oven to 325°F. In ungreased 12x8-inch (2-quart) baking dish, arrange well-drained fruit. In small saucepan, combine remaining ingredients. Heat until margarine is melted. Pour over fruits in baking dish. Bake uncovered at 325°F. for 30 minutes or until hot and bubbly. 8 servings.

■ MICROWAVE DIRECTIONS: In ungreased (2-quart) microwave-safe casserole, arrange well-drained fruit. In 2-cup microwave-safe glass measuring cup, combine margarine and honey. Microwave on HIGH for 1½ to 2 minutes or until margarine is melted. Add curry powder; mix well. Pour over fruits in casserole. Microwave on HIGH for 6 to 7 minutes or until hot and bubbly.

NUTRITION INFORMATION PER SERVING
SERVING SIZE: PERCENT U.S. RDA
1/8 OF RECIPE PER SERVING

CALORIES	210	PROTEIN	2%
PROTEIN	1g	VITAMIN A	25%
CARBOHYDRATE	33g	VITAMIN C	10%
FAT	8g	THIAMINE	6%
CHOLESTEROL	0mg	RIBOFLAVIN	4%
SODIUM	95mg	NIACIN	4%
POTASSIUM	330mg	CALCIUM	2%
		IRON	6%

Curried Fruit Bake

 SIDE DISHES, RELISHES & PRESERVES

COUNTRY COOKING

These unique make-ahead sweet potatoes have a creamy marshmallow filling. They are inspired by a cherished family recipe and could become a family favorite to serve with your Thanksgiving turkey.

Mom's Sweet Potato Puffs

2 lbs. (3 medium) sweet potatoes
¼ teaspoon salt
6 large marshmallows
1 cup finely chopped nuts
1 egg, beaten

In medium saucepan, cook sweet potatoes in boiling water until tender, about 30 to 40 minutes; drain. Peel and mash; stir in salt. Cool slightly. Grease 8 or 9-inch square pan.

Meanwhile, place nuts in ungreased shallow pan. Bake at 350°F. about 10 minutes or until light golden brown, stirring occasionally.

Form ⅙ of potato mixture around each marshmallow, making sure to cover completely. Roll in egg, then nuts; place in prepared pan. Cover with plastic wrap and refrigerate several hours or until ready to bake.

Heat oven to 425°F. Bake uncovered 15 minutes or until outer surface is set and potatoes are thoroughly heated. 6 servings.

NUTRITION INFORMATION PER SERVING

SERVING SIZE: 1 POTATO PUFF		PERCENT U.S. RDA PER SERVING	
CALORIES	290	PROTEIN	8%
PROTEIN	6g	VITAMIN A	440%
CARBOHYDRATE	35g	VITAMIN C	30%
FAT	14g	THIAMINE	10%
CHOLESTEROL	45mg	RIBOFLAVIN	10%
SODIUM	115mg	NIACIN	4%
POTASSIUM	330mg	CALCIUM	4%
		IRON	8%

This colorful salad is made ahead and tossed just before serving. It will be especially appealing to the blue cheese lover!

Layered Cabbage Apple Salad with Blue Cheese Dressing

3 cups (½ small head) finely shredded red cabbage
1 cup seedless green grapes, halved
1 medium red apple, coarsely chopped
¼ cup chopped walnuts
¼ cup sliced green onions

DRESSING*
8-oz. carton (1 cup) plain yogurt
2 oz. (½ cup) crumbled blue cheese
¼ teaspoon garlic salt
1 teaspoon lemon juice

In 2-quart salad bowl, layer cabbage, grapes, apple, walnuts and onions. In small bowl, combine all dressing ingredients. Spoon over salad, spreading to cover. Cover and refrigerate 2 to 3 hours to blend flavors. Toss just before serving. 8 servings.

TIP: *An 8-oz. bottle of blue cheese dressing can be substituted for dressing.

NUTRITION INFORMATION PER SERVING

SERVING SIZE: 1/8 OF RECIPE		PERCENT U.S. RDA PER SERVING	
CALORIES	100	PROTEIN	6%
PROTEIN	4g	VITAMIN A	2%
CARBOHYDRATE	11g	VITAMIN C	30%
FAT	5g	THIAMINE	4%
CHOLESTEROL	6mg	RIBOFLAVIN	6%
SODIUM	180mg	NIACIN	*
POTASSIUM	220mg	CALCIUM	10%
		IRON	*

*Contains less than 2% of the U.S. RDA of this nutrient.

Pictured on previous page, left to right: Mom's Sweet Potato Puffs and Citrus Glazed Ham p. 12

This creamy custard-like mixture is baked in a mold and served as a side dish.

Spinach Timbales

2 (9-oz.) pkg. Green Giant® Harvest Fresh® Frozen Chopped Spinach
6 slices bacon, diced
2 tablespoons chopped onion
½ teaspoon salt
¼ teaspoon pepper
1 cup milk
4 eggs, beaten

Heat oven to 350°F. Grease six 6-oz. custard cups. Cook spinach as directed on package; squeeze to drain. In skillet, cook bacon until crisp (reserve 2 tablespoons drippings). Drain bacon on paper towels. Saute onions in bacon drippings until tender.*

In medium bowl, combine spinach, bacon, onion and remaining ingredients; mix well. Pour into prepared custard cups. Place in 13x9-inch pan. Add hot water to depth of 1 inch. Bake at 350°F. for 45 minutes or until center is set. Unmold onto serving platter.
6 servings.

TIP: *Two tablespoons oil can be substituted for bacon drippings.

NUTRITION INFORMATION PER SERVING
SERVING SIZE: 1 TIMBALE

		PERCENT U.S. RDA PER SERVING	
CALORIES	140	PROTEIN	15%
PROTEIN	10g	VITAMIN A	35%
CARBOHYDRATE	6g	VITAMIN C	6%
FAT	8g	THIAMINE	8%
CHOLESTEROL	190mg	RIBOFLAVIN	20%
SODIUM	660mg	NIACIN	4%
POTASSIUM	490mg	CALCIUM	15%
		IRON	10%

The liquid marinade in the jar of artichokes becomes the marinade for this tangy quick-to-prepare salad.

Brussels Sprout Potato Salad

1 medium (1½ cups) cooked potato, cubed
1 small red bell pepper, cut into ½-inch pieces
9-oz. pkg. frozen brussels sprouts
6-oz. jar marinated artichoke hearts, undrained

In medium saucepan, combine all ingredients. Cook over low heat for 20 minutes or until thoroughly heated, stirring occasionally. Salt and pepper to taste. Serve hot or cold.
6 servings.

■ MICROWAVE DIRECTIONS:
In 1½-quart microwave-safe casserole, combine all ingredients. Cover; microwave on HIGH for 9 to 10 minutes or until thoroughly heated, stirring twice during cooking.

NUTRITION INFORMATION PER SERVING
SERVING SIZE: 1/6 OF RECIPE

		PERCENT U.S. RDA PER SERVING	
CALORIES	100	PROTEIN	4%
PROTEIN	3g	VITAMIN A	15%
CARBOHYDRATE	12g	VITAMIN C	60%
FAT	5g	THIAMINE	6%
CHOLESTEROL	0mg	RIBOFLAVIN	4%
SODIUM	95mg	NIACIN	4%
POTASSIUM	320mg	CALCIUM	2%
		IRON	4%

Turn everyday mashed potatoes into something special.

Onion 'n Chive Mashed Potatoes

1¼ cups water
2 tablespoons margarine or butter
¼ teaspoon garlic salt
¼ cup finely chopped onion
1 tablespoon chopped chives
½ cup milk
½ cup dairy sour cream
1⅓ cups Hungry Jack® Mashed Potato Flakes

In medium saucepan, bring water, margarine, garlic salt, onion and chives to a boil. Remove from heat; stir in milk and sour cream. Add potato flakes, stirring with fork until potatoes are desired consistency. 4 servings.

NUTRITION INFORMATION PER SERVING
SERVING SIZE: 1/4 OF RECIPE

		PERCENT U.S. RDA PER SERVING	
CALORIES	210	PROTEIN	6%
PROTEIN	4g	VITAMIN A	10%
CARBOHYDRATE	19g	VITAMIN C	8%
FAT	13g	THIAMINE	4%
CHOLESTEROL	15mg	RIBOFLAVIN	8%
SODIUM	240mg	NIACIN	2%
POTASSIUM	380mg	CALCIUM	8%
		IRON	*

*Contains less than 2% of the U.S. RDA of this nutrient.

COUNTRY COOKING

Simple Desserts & Sweet Snacks

Simple Desserts & Sweet Snacks
Sweet, satisfying and simply prepared.

In this chapter we invite you to a sampler of updated, choice recipes with old-fashioned flavors in place. Kids will clamor for the special after-school treats and the festive fall party ideas like **Jack-O'-Lantern Tarts** and **Halloween Party Pops.** For the adults, the delicately-flavored **Poached Pears with Raspberry Sauce** is an elegant ending to a hearty harvest meal. Pears for cooking, by the way, should be firm, bruise-free and just ripe for shapely, flavorful results. And among these prized recipes, many feature the favorite fruit of fall harvest, apples.

"A" is definitely for "apple." This appealing, all-purpose fruit is prized for great taste, versatility and high-fiber content. Although we would love to claim apples as native American, the fact is the first varieties were cultivated back in the Stone Age. Roman orchards around 400 A.D. boasted over two dozen types and the lore of this most useful fruit and the beauty of its blossoms have been subjects of legends, poems and other classical writings for centuries.

Early American tables featured apple dishes almost every day for every meal and cider presses were seldom idle. Today the U.S. is one of the world's leading producers, and American breeders have made noteworthy progress in developing varieties which are disease and weather-resistant as well as hardy enough to survive commercial handling and shipping. Although over 7,000 distinct types exist, most of us have access to about 18 varieties.

How does one choose from the array? For just the right apple for every use, you'll find helpful guidelines on pages 89 and 90.

Pictured on previous page:
Gingerbread Tarts with
Fruit and Honey Cream

Enjoy the great taste of ever-popular gingerbread cookies in these individual tarts.

Gingerbread Tarts with Fruit and Honey Cream

CRUST

- 3 tablespoons firmly packed brown sugar
- ¼ cup margarine or butter, softened
- 3 tablespoons molasses
- 1 egg
- 1½ cups Pillsbury's BEST® All Purpose or Unbleached Flour
- ½ teaspoon ginger
- ½ teaspoon allspice
- ¼ teaspoon salt

FILLING

- 2 small red apples, cut into bite-sized pieces
- 2 kiwifruit, peeled, sliced
- 11-oz. can mandarin oranges, drained

TOPPING

- 1 cup whipping cream
- ¼ teaspoon cinnamon
- 2 tablespoons honey

In large bowl, beat brown sugar and margarine until light and fluffy. Add molasses and egg; blend well. Lightly spoon flour into measuring cup; level off. Stir in flour, ginger, allspice and salt; mix well. If necessary, chill for easier handling.

Heat oven to 350°F. Grease back sides of 10 muffin cups. On lightly floured surface, roll dough to ⅛-inch thickness. Cut dough with 4-inch, fluted, round, floured cookie cutter or knife and paper pattern. Reroll dough scraps for more rounds. Form over backs of prepared muffin cups, pleating to fit snugly. Bake 10 minutes or until firm. Remove from muffin cups; cool on wire rack.

In small bowl, combine filling ingredients; spoon into cooled tart shells. In small bowl, beat topping ingredients until soft peaks form. Spoon over fruit. 10 to 12 tarts.

NUTRITION INFORMATION PER SERVING

SERVING SIZE: 1/12 OF RECIPE		PERCENT U.S. RDA PER SERVING	
CALORIES	240	PROTEIN	4%
PROTEIN	3g	VITAMIN A	10%
CARBOHYDRATE	29g	VITAMIN C	15%
FAT	12g	THIAMINE	8%
CHOLESTEROL	50mg	RIBOFLAVIN	6%
SODIUM	105mg	NIACIN	6%
POTASSIUM	210mg	CALCIUM	4%
		IRON	8%

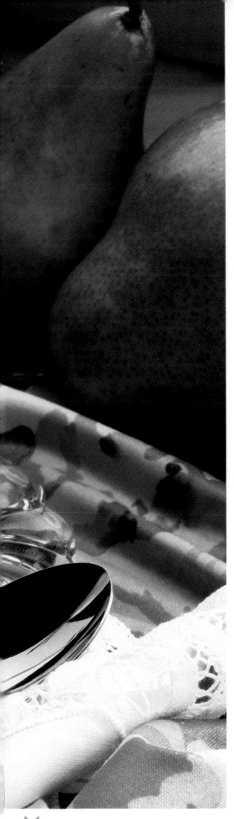

With very little effort you can create this elegant, light dessert.

Poached Pears with Raspberry Sauce

    4 medium ripe pears
       Lemon juice
  ½ cup sugar
    1 teaspoon grated lemon peel
    3 whole cloves
    1 cinnamon stick
    4 cups water
10-oz. pkg. frozen raspberries in
       syrup, thawed

Peel pears; remove core from bottom and leave stems attached. Brush pears with lemon juice. In large kettle, combine sugar, lemon peel, cloves, cinnamon stick and water. Bring to a boil; add pears in upright position. Reduce heat; cover and simmer 20 to 25 minutes or until pears are tender. Chill pears in poaching liquid.

Meanwhile, force raspberries through sieve to remove seeds. Chill. To serve, place pears upright in individual dessert dishes. Spoon raspberry sauce over each pear. 4 servings.

MICROWAVE DIRECTIONS: Prepare pears as directed above. In 9 or 10-inch round microwave-safe dish or pie plate, combine sugar, lemon peel, cloves, cinnamon stick and ½ **cup** water. Microwave on HIGH for 3 to 4 minutes or until mixture boils. Place pears upright in dish; baste with syrup. Cover with plastic wrap. Microwave on HIGH for 12 to 16 minutes or until pears are tender, basting occasionally with syrup. Continue as directed above.

NUTRITION INFORMATION PER SERVING

SERVING SIZE: 1/4 OF RECIPE		PERCENT U.S. RDA PER SERVING	
CALORIES	250	PROTEIN	*
PROTEIN	1g	VITAMIN A	*
CARBOHYDRATE	60g	VITAMIN C	20%
FAT	1g	THIAMINE	2%
CHOLESTEROL	0mg	RIBOFLAVIN	4%
SODIUM	0mg	NIACIN	*
POTASSIUM	270mg	CALCIUM	2%
		IRON	4%

*Contains less than 2% of the U.S. RDA of this nutrient.

Apple pies are considered an American specialty, however, this unique version was inspired by France's Tarte Tatin.

Upside-Down Apple Pie

NUTRITION INFORMATION PER SERVING

SERVING SIZE: 1/8 OF RECIPE		PERCENT U.S. RDA PER SERVING	
CALORIES	510	PROTEIN	2%
PROTEIN	2g	VITAMIN A	6%
CARBOHYDRATE	66g	VITAMIN C	6%
FAT	26g	THIAMINE	6%
CHOLESTEROL	0mg	RIBOFLAVIN	2%
SODIUM	460mg	NIACIN	2%
POTASSIUM	180mg	CALCIUM	2%
		IRON	2%

GLAZE

 2 tablespoons margarine or butter
½ cup pecan or walnut halves
⅓ cup firmly packed brown sugar

  Pastry for 9-inch two-crust pie

FILLING

 6 cups sliced, peeled apples
¾ cup sugar
 2 tablespoons flour
¼ teaspoon salt
 2 tablespoons lemon juice
 2 tablespoons margarine or butter

Line 9-inch pie pan with 13-inch circle of foil; do not trim excess foil. Spread 2 tablespoons margarine over foil in bottom and up sides of pan. Place pecan halves, rounded sides down, in bottom of prepared pan. Sprinkle brown sugar over pecans.

Heat oven to 450°F. Prepare desired pastry for two-crust pie. Gently ease pastry into prepared pan over pecan-brown sugar mixture. In large bowl, combine apples, sugar, flour, salt and lemon juice; mix lightly. Spoon into pastry-lined pan; dot with 2 tablespoons margarine. Top with remaining pastry; fold edge of top pastry under bottom pastry. Seal edges together securely. Cut several slits in top crust for steam to escape. Fold excess foil loosely over edge of pastry to prevent excessive browning. Bake at 450°F. for 10 minutes. Reduce oven temperature to 375°F.; continue baking for 30 to 40 minutes or until apples are tender and crust is golden brown. (Place pan on foil or cookie sheet during baking to guard against spillage.) Cool pie upright in pan for 5 minutes; invert onto serving plate. Cool at least 1 hour before serving; serve warm. 8 servings.

A warm, rich, creamy sauce to use in so many ways. Spoon it over warm gingerbread squares or over Caramel Apples-in-a-Bowl.

Caramel Sauce

½ cup butter or margarine
1½ cups firmly packed brown sugar
 2 tablespoons light corn syrup
½ cup whipping cream

MICROWAVE DIRECTIONS:
In 4-cup microwave-safe glass measuring cup, melt butter on HIGH for 1 to 1½ minutes. Stir in brown sugar and syrup. Microwave on HIGH for 3 to 3½ minutes or until mixture boils, stirring after every minute. Stir in whipping cream. Microwave on HIGH for 1 to 1½ minutes or until mixture boils. Cool to room temperature. Store in refrigerator. 2 cups.

CONVENTIONAL DIRECTIONS:
In medium saucepan, melt butter. Stir in brown sugar and syrup. Bring to a boil; cook until sugar is dissolved, stirring constantly. Stir in whipping cream and bring to a boil again. Remove from heat. Serve warm. Store in refrigerator.

NUTRITION INFORMATION PER SERVING

SERVING SIZE: 1 TABLESPOON		PERCENT U.S. RDA PER SERVING	
CALORIES	80	PROTEIN	*
PROTEIN	0g	VITAMIN A	2%
CARBOHYDRATE	11g	VITAMIN C	*
FAT	4g	THIAMINE	*
CHOLESTEROL	10mg	RIBOFLAVIN	*
SODIUM	35mg	NIACIN	*
POTASSIUM	40mg	CALCIUM	*
		IRON	2%

*Contains less than 2% of the U.S. RDA of this nutrient.

Spicy and delicious for cool weather.

Streusel-Topped Gingerbread with Butter Sauce

½ cup sugar
¼ cup margarine or butter, softened
1 cup Pillsbury's BEST® All Purpose or Unbleached Flour
1 teaspoon ginger
1 teaspoon cinnamon
½ teaspoon allspice
⅛ teaspoon salt
½ teaspoon baking soda
½ cup buttermilk*
¼ cup molasses
1 egg, slightly beaten

BUTTER SAUCE
½ cup sugar
Dash ginger
¼ cup butter or margarine
¼ cup whipping cream

Heat oven to 375°F. Grease bottom only of 8-inch square pan or 8-inch round cake pan. In large bowl, combine ½ cup sugar and ¼ cup margarine; blend well. Lightly spoon flour into measuring cup; level off. Add flour, 1 teaspoon ginger, cinnamon, allspice and salt; mix until crumbly. Reserve ⅓ cup of mixture for topping. To remaining mixture, add baking soda; mix well. Add buttermilk, molasses and egg; blend well. Pour batter into greased pan; sprinkle with reserved mixture. Bake at 375°F. for 20 to 30 minutes or until toothpick inserted in center comes out clean.

In small saucepan, combine all sauce ingredients. Bring to a boil over medium heat, stirring constantly. Reduce heat; simmer 4 minutes, stirring occasionally. Serve warm sauce over gingerbread. Refrigerate any remaining sauce. 9 servings.

TIP: *To substitute for buttermilk, use 1½ teaspoons vinegar or lemon juice plus milk to make ½ cup.

HIGH ALTITUDE—Above 3500 Feet: Increase flour to 1⅓ cups. Bake as directed above.

NUTRITION INFORMATION PER SERVING
SERVING SIZE: 1/9 OF RECIPE

		PERCENT U.S. RDA PER SERVING	
CALORIES	290	PROTEIN	4%
PROTEIN	3g	VITAMIN A	10%
CARBOHYDRATE	40g	VITAMIN C	*
FAT	14g	THIAMINE	8%
CHOLESTEROL	47mg	RIBOFLAVIN	8%
SODIUM	230mg	NIACIN	4%
POTASSIUM	150mg	CALCIUM	6%
		IRON	8%

*Contains less than 2% of the U.S. RDA of this nutrient.

A fun, tasty way to give your family a nutritious treat.

Caramel Apples-in-a-Bowl

2 apples, cut into bite-sized pieces
1 banana, peeled and sliced
¼ cup chopped peanuts
¾ cup Caramel Sauce

Spoon apples, banana and peanuts into 4 dessert dishes. Pour Caramel Sauce over fruits. 4 servings.

NUTRITION INFORMATION PER SERVING
SERVING SIZE: 1/4 OF RECIPE

		PERCENT U.S. RDA PER SERVING	
CALORIES	370	PROTEIN	4%
PROTEIN	3g	VITAMIN A	10%
CARBOHYDRATE	52g	VITAMIN C	10%
FAT	17g	THIAMINE	2%
CHOLESTEROL	40mg	RIBOFLAVIN	2%
SODIUM	135mg	NIACIN	6%
POTASSIUM	370mg	CALCIUM	4%
		IRON	8%

The mouth-watering down-home-style baked apples bake in just minutes in the microwave.

Saucy Microwave Baked Apples

4 medium apples
4 tablespoons brown sugar
4 tablespoons raisins
4 tablespoons margarine or butter

▣ MICROWAVE DIRECTIONS:
Core apples and cut 1-inch strip of peel around top to prevent splitting. Place apples in ungreased 9-inch microwave-safe pie plate. Spoon brown sugar and raisins into center of each apple; top with margarine. Cover with microwave-safe plastic wrap. Microwave on HIGH for 6 to 8 minutes or until tender, rotating dish ½ turn halfway through cooking. Spoon brown sugar mixture over apples. 4 servings.

NUTRITION INFORMATION PER SERVING

SERVING SIZE: 1/4 OF RECIPE		PERCENT U.S. RDA PER SERVING	
CALORIES	280	PROTEIN	*
PROTEIN	1g	VITAMIN A	10%
CARBOHYDRATE	42g	VITAMIN C	15%
FAT	12g	THIAMINE	2%
CHOLESTEROL	0mg	RIBOFLAVIN	*
SODIUM	140mg	NIACIN	*
POTASSIUM	280mg	CALCIUM	2%
		IRON	4%

*Contains less than 2% of the U.S. RDA of this nutrient.

Enjoy fall's abundance of apples in this wonderful dessert.

Apple Bread Pudding with Vanilla Sauce

PUDDING
4 cups soft whole wheat or white bread cubes
2 cups thinly sliced, peeled apples
¼ cup raisins
1 cup firmly packed brown sugar
1¾ cups milk
¼ cup margarine or butter
1 teaspoon cinnamon
½ teaspoon vanilla
2 eggs, beaten

SAUCE
½ cup sugar
½ cup brown sugar
½ cup whipping cream
½ cup margarine or butter
1 teaspoon vanilla

Heat oven to 350°F. Grease 10x6-inch (1½-quart) baking dish. In large bowl, combine bread, apples and raisins. In small saucepan, combine 1 cup brown sugar, milk and ¼ cup margarine. Cook over medium heat until margarine is melted; pour over bread mixture in bowl. Let stand 10 minutes. Stir in cinnamon, ½ teaspoon vanilla and eggs. Pour into prepared baking dish. Bake at 350°F. for 40 to 50 minutes or until center is set and apples are tender.

In small saucepan, combine sugar, ½ cup brown sugar, whipping cream and ½ cup margarine. Cook over medium heat until mixture boils, stirring occasionally. Stir in vanilla. Serve warm over pudding. 8 servings.

NUTRITION INFORMATION PER SERVING

SERVING SIZE: 1/8 OF RECIPE		PERCENT U.S. RDA PER SERVING	
CALORIES	550	PROTEIN	10%
PROTEIN	6g	VITAMIN A	20%
CARBOHYDRATE	74g	VITAMIN C	2%
FAT	26g	THIAMINE	6%
CHOLESTEROL	90mg	RIBOFLAVIN	10%
SODIUM	380mg	NIACIN	4%
POTASSIUM	390mg	CALCIUM	15%
		IRON	15%

Saucy Microwave Baked Apples

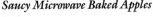

These whimsical cookies on a stick are simple to make and fun to eat. Children will love to help decorate them; let your imaginations run wild.

Halloween Party Pops

20-oz. pkg. Pillsbury's BEST® Refrigerated Sugar Cookies
20 wooden sticks

Freeze cookie dough for 1 hour or longer. Heat oven to 350°F. Cut frozen dough into about twenty ½-inch slices. Roll each into a ball. Arrange in circle on ungreased cookie sheets, 3 inches apart and 2 inches from edges. Securely insert a wooden stick into each ball with end pointing toward center of cookie sheet. Bake at 350°F. for 10 to 14 minutes or until golden brown. Cool 2 minutes; remove from cookie sheet with spatula. Cool completely. Use the following frostings or Pillsbury Frosting Supreme Ready To Spread Frostings to frost or decorate as desired. 20 cookie pops.

WHITE FROSTING

1 cup powdered sugar
1 tablespoon milk
1 tablespoon margarine or butter, softened

In small bowl, combine all ingredients; blend until smooth. If necessary, add additional milk 1 drop at a time for desired consistency. About ½ cup frosting.

TIP: For orange colored frosting, add 2 drops yellow food coloring and 1 drop red food coloring.

CHOCOLATE FROSTING

1 cup powdered sugar
2 tablespoons cocoa
1 to 2 tablespoons milk
1 tablespoon margarine or butter, softened

In small bowl, combine all ingredients; blend until smooth. If necessary, add additional milk 1 drop at a time for desired consistency. About ½ cup frosting.

Decorating ideas:

BLACK CAT
Slice a large black gumdrop into 3 round pieces. Use small end for head; use largest piece for body. Cut ears and tail from third piece. Frost cookie with orange frosting. Arrange gumdrop pieces on frosted cookie to form cat.

SPIDER WEB
Frost cookie with chocolate frosting. Pipe white frosting over chocolate in spiral pattern starting from center. Using toothpick or fork, draw lines outward through frostings starting at center of cookie.

JACK-O'-LANTERNS, CATS, OWLS, GHOSTS, ETC.
Frost cookies. Use candies such as gum drops, candy corn and licorice to create desired party pop characters.

NUTRITION INFORMATION PER SERVING			
SERVING SIZE:		PERCENT U.S. RDA	
1 COOKIE POP		PER SERVING	
CALORIES	140	PROTEIN	*
PROTEIN	1g	VITAMIN A	*
CARBOHYDRATE	23g	VITAMIN C	*
FAT	5g	THIAMINE	4%
CHOLESTEROL	0mg	RIBOFLAVIN	6%
SODIUM	125mg	NIACIN	2%
POTASSIUM	50mg	CALCIUM	*
		IRON	2%

*Contains less than 2% of the U.S. RDA of this nutrient.

Halloween Party Pops

Two family favorites are combined in one mouth-watering dessert. Serve warm from the oven for delicious home-baked goodness.

Country Pineapple Gingerbread

¼ cup margarine or butter
½ cup firmly packed brown sugar
2 (8¼-oz.) cans sliced pineapple, drained
8 pecan or walnut halves
½ cup firmly packed brown sugar
½ cup margarine or butter, softened
½ cup molasses
½ cup water
2 eggs
1¾ cups Pillsbury's BEST® All Purpose or Unbleached Flour
1 teaspoon baking soda
1 teaspoon cinnamon
1 teaspoon ginger
¼ teaspoon allspice
Whipped cream

Heat oven to 350°F. In heavy 10-inch ovenproof skillet, melt ¼ cup margarine. Add ½ cup brown sugar; stir until melted. Arrange pineapple slices over mixture; place pecan halves in centers. In large bowl, cream ½ cup brown sugar and ½ cup margarine until light and fluffy. Add molasses, water and eggs; mix well. Lightly spoon flour into measuring cup; level off. Gradually add flour, baking soda, cinnamon, ginger and allspice until well mixed; pour evenly over pineapple. Bake at 350°F. for 30 to 40 minutes or until toothpick inserted in center comes out clean. Cool 5 minutes; loosen edges and invert onto serving plate. Serve warm or cool with whipped cream. 8 servings.

TIP: A 12x8-inch (2-quart) baking dish can be substituted for skillet. Melt margarine in baking dish in oven. Remove from oven; stir in brown sugar. Prepare and bake as directed above.

HIGH ALTITUDE—Above 3500 Feet: Increase water to ½ cup plus 2 tablespoons and flour to 2 cups. Bake at 375°F. for 30 to 40 minutes.

NUTRITION INFORMATION PER SERVING

SERVING SIZE: 1/8 OF RECIPE		PERCENT U.S. RDA PER SERVING	
CALORIES	480	PROTEIN	8%
PROTEIN	5g	VITAMIN A	20%
CARBOHYDRATE	66g	VITAMIN C	4%
FAT	22g	THIAMINE	20%
CHOLESTEROL	80mg	RIBOFLAVIN	10%
SODIUM	380mg	NIACIN	10%
POTASSIUM	450mg	CALCIUM	10%
		IRON	20%

Two favorite flavors combined in one forever-popular bar.

Chocolate Peanut Butter Crispy Rice Bars

¼ cup margarine or butter
10-oz. pkg. (about 40) regular marshmallows or 4 cups miniature marshmallows
6 cups ready-sweetened chocolate-flavored rice cereal
1 cup peanut butter chips
½ cup chopped peanuts, if desired

Grease 13x9-inch pan. In large saucepan, melt margarine and marshmallows over low heat, stirring occasionally. Remove from heat; stir in cereal, peanut butter chips and peanuts until well-coated. Press mixture into prepared pan. Cool. Cut into bars. 36 bars.

NUTRITION INFORMATION PER SERVING

SERVING SIZE: 1 BAR		PERCENT U.S. RDA PER SERVING	
CALORIES	100	PROTEIN	2%
PROTEIN	2g	VITAMIN A	6%
CARBOHYDRATE	14g	VITAMIN C	4%
FAT	4g	THIAMINE	6%
CHOLESTEROL	0mg	RIBOFLAVIN	6%
SODIUM	85mg	NIACIN	8%
POTASSIUM	50mg	CALCIUM	*
		IRON	2%

*Contains less than 2% of the U.S. RDA of this nutrient.

Pictured left to right: Chocolate Peanut Butter Crispy Rice Bars and Cranberry Apple Gelatin Cut-Outs p. 89

These rich and chocolaty sweet treats are sure to be a hit with all those ghosts and goblins. They're a snap to prepare with refrigerated sugar cookie dough.

Jack-O'-Lantern Tarts

TART
20-oz. pkg. Pillsbury's BEST® Refrigerated Sugar Cookies
3½-oz. pkg. chocolate pudding and pie filling, prepared according to package directions and chilled
2 (11-oz.) cans mandarin orange segments, drained

FROSTING*
½ cup powdered sugar
1½ to 2 teaspoons milk
1 drop yellow food coloring
1 drop green food coloring

Freeze cookie dough for 1 hour or longer. Heat oven to 325°F. Grease 12 muffin cups. Slice twelve ¼-inch slices from frozen cookie dough.** Place in bottom of prepared muffin cups. Bake at 325°F. for 12 to 15 minutes or until golden brown around edges. Cool 2 minutes; remove from muffin cups. Cool completely.

To assemble each tart, top cookie with 1 to 2 tablespoons pudding. (Pudding will be left over.) Arrange 4 to 5 orange segments side-by-side with outer curved surface facing upward as if putting orange back together on top of pudding.

In small bowl, combine powdered sugar and milk; mix well. If needed, add additional milk 1 drop at a time to achieve desired consistency. Divide into 2 bowls. To one, stir in yellow food coloring; to the other, green food coloring. Decorate tarts to resemble jack-o'-lanterns. Use toothpicks to apply green frosting for the stem and yellow frosting for the eyes, nose and mouth. 12 tarts.

TIPS: *Pillsbury Decorator Icing— Yellow and Green—can be substituted for frosting.
**Prepare remaining cookie dough as directed on package.

NUTRITION INFORMATION PER SERVING			
SERVING SIZE: 1 TART		PERCENT U.S. RDA PER SERVING	
CALORIES	280	PROTEIN	6%
PROTEIN	4g	VITAMIN A	8%
CARBOHYDRATE	47g	VITAMIN C	20%
FAT	9g	THIAMINE	10%
CHOLESTEROL	2mg	RIBOFLAVIN	15%
SODIUM	250mg	NIACIN	6%
POTASSIUM	200mg	CALCIUM	6%
		IRON	6%

When Mom made pie, my sister and I always waited anxiously for the cinnamon and sugar cut-outs she made with the leftover dough. With All Ready Pie Crusts you can have those same delightful treats in a jiffy. For a great soup topper, sprinkle the cut-outs with cheese before baking.

Pie Crust Cut-Outs

15-oz. pkg. Pillsbury All Ready Pie Crusts
1 teaspoon flour

FLAVORFUL TOPPINGS
Sugar
Colored sugar
Cinnamon-sugar mixture:
1 tablespoon sugar plus ¼ teaspoon cinnamon
Colored or chocolate sprinkles
Garlic or onion salt
Grated American cheese
Cheesy-seasoning mixture:
1 tablespoon grated Parmesan cheese plus ½ teaspoon Italian or Mexican seasoning

Allow 1 pie crust pouch to stand at room temperature for 15 to 20 minutes. (Refrigerate remaining crust for later use.) Heat oven to 400°F. Unfold pie crust; peel off top plastic sheet. Press out fold lines; sprinkle flour over crust. Turn crust, flour side down, on cutting board or pastry cloth; peel off remaining plastic sheet.

Using 2-inch floured cutters, cut out desired shapes.* Place 1 inch apart on ungreased cookie sheet. Reroll trimmings, if desired. Sprinkle cutouts with desired toppings. Bake at 400°F. for 6 to 9 minutes or until light golden brown. Remove from pan; cool completely. Store in loosely covered container. 32 snacks.

TIP: *To use as a soup topper, cut with 1-inch floured cutters. Decrease bake time to 5 minutes or until light golden brown.

NUTRITION INFORMATION PER SERVING
SERVING SIZE: 1 SNACK   PERCENT U.S. RDA
WITH CINNAMON-   PER SERVING
SUGAR TOPPING   PROTEIN   *
CALORIES   30   VITAMIN A   *
PROTEIN   0g   VITAMIN C   *
CARBOHYDRATE   3g   THIAMINE   *
FAT   2g   RIBOFLAVIN   *
CHOLESTEROL   0mg   NIACIN   *
SODIUM   40mg   CALCIUM   *
POTASSIUM   0mg   IRON   *
*Contains less than 2% of the U.S. RDA of this nutrient.

These colorful sweet treats with flavor-filled candies, crispy cereal puffs and gooey marshmallows are sure to be a hit with the kids.

Cereal Balls

6 cups crispy corn puff cereal
½ cup raisins
10¾-oz. bag spiced jelly candies
¼ cup margarine or butter
10-oz. pkg. (about 40) regular marshmallows or 4 cups miniature marshmallows

In large bowl, combine cereal, raisins and candies. In large saucepan, melt margarine and marshmallows over low heat, stirring occasionally. Pour over cereal mixture; stir quickly to coat. With wet hands, quickly shape mixture into 12 balls. Place on waxed paper; cool. Store in tightly covered container. 12 balls.

NUTRITION INFORMATION PER SERVING
SERVING SIZE: PERCENT U.S. RDA
1 BALL   PER SERVING
CALORIES   260   PROTEIN   2%
PROTEIN   2g   VITAMIN A   20%
CARBOHYDRATE   54g   VITAMIN C   15%
FAT   4g   THIAMINE   15%
CHOLESTEROL   0mg   RIBOFLAVIN   15%
SODIUM   270mg   NIACIN   15%
POTASSIUM   75mg   CALCIUM   2%
                             IRON   30%

The harvest time bounty of apples and cranberries becomes a delicious combination in this not-so-sweet dessert.

Cranberry Apple Crisp

5 cups peeled, sliced apples
1½ cups fresh or frozen chopped cranberries
1 cup sugar
2 tablespoons flour
1 teaspoon cinnamon
1 cup quick-cooking rolled oats
½ cup firmly packed brown sugar
⅓ cup flour
¼ cup margarine or butter
½ cup chopped nuts
Whipped cream

Heat oven to 375°F. Grease 12x8-inch (2-quart) baking dish. In large bowl, combine apples, cranberries, sugar, 2 tablespoons flour and cinnamon. Spoon into prepared baking dish. In small bowl, combine rolled oats, brown sugar and ⅓ cup flour. Cut in margarine with pastry blender or fork until consistency of coarse meal. Stir in nuts. Sprinkle crumb mixture evenly over fruit. Bake at 375°F. for 30 to 40 minutes or until golden brown and apples are tender. Serve with whipped cream. 10 servings.

🖳 MICROWAVE DIRECTIONS: In large bowl, combine apples, cranberries, sugar, **3 tablespoons** flour and cinnamon. Spoon into ungreased 12x8-inch (2-quart) microwave-safe casserole. In small bowl, combine rolled oats, brown sugar, ⅓ cup flour, **melted** margarine and nuts; mix well. Sprinkle crumb mixture evenly over fruit. Microwave on HIGH for 10 to 12 minutes or until apples are tender, rotating dish ½ turn halfway through cooking.

NUTRITION INFORMATION PER SERVING
SERVING SIZE: PERCENT U.S. RDA
1/10 OF RECIPE   PER SERVING
CALORIES   330   PROTEIN   4%
PROTEIN   3g   VITAMIN A   15%
CARBOHYDRATE   52g   VITAMIN C   6%
FAT   12g   THIAMINE   15%
CHOLESTEROL   10mg   RIBOFLAVIN   8%
SODIUM   140mg   NIACIN   10%
POTASSIUM   190mg   CALCIUM   6%
                             IRON   15%

Reminiscent of apple pie, this is a new twist of that old favorite. You don't even need a pie pan.

Maple Frosted Apple Pan-Tart

15-oz. pkg. Pillsbury All Ready Pie
    Crusts
  1 teaspoon flour
1½ cups cornflakes cereal
  6 cups peeled, thinly sliced
    apples
  1 cup sugar
  1 teaspoon cinnamon
  1 egg white, beaten

GLAZE
  ½ cup powdered sugar
  3 tablespoons maple-flavored
    syrup

Heat oven to 350°F. Allow both crust pouches to sit at room temperature for 15 to 20 minutes. Unfold one pie crust; peel off top plastic sheet. Press out fold lines; sprinkle flour over crust. Turn crust, flour side down, on ungreased cookie sheet; peel off remaining plastic sheet. Sprinkle cornflakes over crust to within ½ inch of edge. Top with apples; sprinkle with 1 cup sugar and cinnamon. Brush edge of crust with egg white. Unfold second crust; peel off plastic sheets. Press out fold lines; place over filling. Fold edge of bottom crust over top crust; pinch and flute edges to seal. Cut several slits in top crust for steam to escape; brush with beaten egg white. Bake at 350°F. for 45 to 55 minutes or until golden brown and apples are tender.

In small bowl, combine glaze ingredients. Drizzle over warm crust. To serve, cut into wedges. Serve warm or cold. 8 servings.

NUTRITION INFORMATION PER SERVING

SERVING SIZE: 1/8 OF RECIPE		PERCENT U.S. RDA PER SERVING	
CALORIES	460	PROTEIN	2%
PROTEIN	2g	VITAMIN A	4%
CARBOHYDRATE	76g	VITAMIN C	6%
FAT	16g	THIAMINE	4%
CHOLESTEROL	0mg	RIBOFLAVIN	4%
SODIUM	380mg	NIACIN	4%
POTASSIUM	130mg	CALCIUM	*
		IRON	2%

*Contains less than 2% of the U.S. RDA of this nutrient.

Whether a special occasion or simply coffee in the afternoon, it always called for a plate of cookies at Grandma's house. Thumbprints were a favorite. The color of frosting varied depending upon the season or holiday.

Grandma's Thumbprints

COOKIES
- ½ cup firmly packed brown sugar
- 1 cup margarine or butter, softened
- 2 eggs, separated
- 2 cups Pillsbury's BEST® All Purpose or Unbleached Flour
- ⅛ teaspoon salt
- 1½ cups finely chopped pecans

FROSTING
- 2 cups powdered sugar
- ⅛ teaspoon salt
- 3 tablespoons margarine or butter, softened
- 1 to 2 tablespoons milk
- ½ teaspoon vanilla
  Food coloring*

Heat oven to 325°F. Lightly grease cookie sheets. In large bowl, beat brown sugar and 1 cup margarine until light and fluffy. Add egg yolks; blend well. Lightly spoon flour into measuring cup; level off. Stir in flour and ⅛ teaspoon salt; mix well.

In small bowl, lightly beat egg whites. Shape dough into ¾-inch balls. Dip in egg whites; roll in nuts. Place 2 inches apart on prepared cookie sheets. With thumb, make imprint in center of each cookie. Bake at 325°F. for 12 to 15 minutes or until edges are light golden brown. Cool slightly; remove from cookie sheets.

In small bowl, combine all frosting ingredients until smooth. Spoon or pipe into center of each cookie.
5½ dozen cookies.

TIP: *For chocolate frosting, omit food coloring and add 2 tablespoons cocoa.

HIGH ALTITUDE—Above 3500 Feet: No change.

NUTRITION INFORMATION PER SERVING			
SERVING SIZE:		PERCENT U.S. RDA	
1 COOKIE		PER SERVING	
CALORIES	80	PROTEIN	*
PROTEIN	1g	VITAMIN A	2%
CARBOHYDRATE	8g	VITAMIN C	*
FAT	5g	THIAMINE	2%
CHOLESTEROL	8mg	RIBOFLAVIN	*
SODIUM	50mg	NIACIN	*
POTASSIUM	25mg	CALCIUM	*
		IRON	*

*Contains less than 2% of the U.S. RDA of this nutrient.

This old-fashioned favorite has been greatly simplified by using refrigerated all ready pie crusts. It is absolutely delicious served warm with cream.

Apple Dumplings

- 15-oz. pkg. Pillsbury All Ready Pie Crusts
- 4 Jonathan, Winesap or other small (2½-inch diameter) baking apples, peeled and cored*
- ¼ cup sugar
- 1 teaspoon cinnamon
- 2 tablespoons raisins
- 1 egg
- 1 teaspoon water

SAUCE
- ½ cup sugar
- 1 cup water
- 2 tablespoons margarine or butter
- ¼ teaspoon cinnamon

Heat oven to 400°F. Allow 1 crust pouch to sit at room temperature 15 to 20 minutes. (Refrigerate remaining crust for later use.) Unfold pie crust; peel off plastic sheets. Cut crust into fourths. From curved edge of each pastry piece, cut a leaf shape to use as garnish.

Place an apple in center of each pastry piece. In small bowl, combine ¼ cup sugar, 1 teaspoon cinnamon and raisins; spoon ¼ mixture into apple cavity. Bring sides of pastry piece up to top of apple; press edges to seal. Garnish with pastry leaf. Place in ungreased 9-inch square baking pan.

Repeat with remaining apples. In small bowl, beat together egg and 1 teaspoon water; brush over dumplings. Bake at 400°F. for 15 minutes.

Meanwhile, in small saucepan combine all sauce ingredients. Bring to a boil; continue boiling for 2 minutes. Pour over partially baked dumplings; bake for an additional 25 to 30 minutes or until crust is deep golden brown and apples are tender. Spoon sauce over dumplings several times during baking. Serve warm or cool. 4 dumplings.

TIP: *If larger baking apples are used, cut in half horizontally. Place apple half on pastry piece, cut side down.

NUTRITION INFORMATION PER SERVING
SERVING SIZE:
1 DUMPLING

		PERCENT U.S. RDA PER SERVING	
CALORIES	530	PROTEIN	4%
PROTEIN	3g	VITAMIN A	6%
CARBOHYDRATE	80g	VITAMIN C	6%
FAT	23g	THIAMINE	2%
CHOLESTEROL	70mg	RIBOFLAVIN	2%
SODIUM	410mg	NIACIN	*
POTASSIUM	190mg	CALCIUM	2%
		IRON	4%

*Contains less than 2% of the U.S. RDA of this nutrient.

These delightful cut-outs are cool, tart and refreshing! Kids will enjoy picking them up to eat with their fingers.

Cranberry Apple Gelatin Cut-Outs

12-oz. can frozen cranberry juice concentrate, thawed
1½ cups apple juice
3 envelopes unflavored gelatin

Lightly grease 13x9-inch pan. In medium saucepan, combine juices. Sprinkle gelatin over top; allow to soften 1 to 2 minutes. Bring to a boil over medium-high heat. Stir constantly to dissolve gelatin. Pour into prepared pan. Refrigerate until firm. Cut into desired shapes with cookie cutters or cut into squares. 48 squares.

NUTRITION INFORMATION PER SERVING
SERVING SIZE:
1 SQUARE

		PERCENT U.S. RDA PER SERVING	
CALORIES	20	PROTEIN	*
PROTEIN	0g	VITAMIN A	*
CARBOHYDRATE	5g	VITAMIN C	2%
FAT	0g	THIAMINE	*
CHOLESTEROL	0mg	RIBOFLAVIN	*
SODIUM	0mg	NIACIN	*
POTASSIUM	15mg	CALCIUM	*
		IRON	*

*Contains less than 2% of the U.S. RDA of this nutrient.

COOK'S NOTE *All About Apples*

- *Begin by selecting a variety best suited to your purpose from the Apple Selection Guide, page 90.*
- *Choose firm, blemish-free apples with a smooth skin, good color and pleasant aroma. If skin has a waxy coating, scrub gently with a vegetable brush under warm water; do not soak.*
- *Apples can be stored at room temperature for brief periods. However, for longer periods, they keep best in a cool, dry, dark spot or in the refrigerator. Apples continue to ripen after picking, thus the need for cooler temperatures to retain crisp texture and tart flavor.*

- *For baking, apples should be tart, juicy and firm enough so slices or pieces retain their shape throughout cooking for attractive presentation.*
- *For sauce, choose apples that are tart and juicy; shape retention is usually unimportant.*
- *Apples to be eaten raw and used in salads should be flavorful, juicy and tender with less acidity than their cooking cousins.*
- *Pare apples as close to eating or cooking time as possible and avoid discoloration by brushing cut surfaces with citrus juice or vinegar.*

Because many of our recipes feature apples, we include this guide to help you choose the best readily-available varieties for eating and cooking purposes. If your area features apples not mentioned here, consult your grocer regarding best uses.

APPLE SELECTION GUIDE

VARIETY	ATTRIBUTES	SUGGESTED USES
Baldwin	Small size. Firm with mild, tart flavor.	All-purpose.
Cortland	Medium to large size. Crisp and juicy with a sweet/tart taste.	All-purpose. Well suited to eating fresh because it is slow to discolor.
Delicious, Golden	Very popular. Sweet with excellent flavor and texture.	All-purpose. Well suited to salads because it doesn't darken after cutting.
Delicious, Red	A favorite due to crisp texture, sweet flavor and bright red color.	Eating raw/salads. Not recommended for cooking.
Granny Smith	Firm texture, green-skinned. Quite juicy and tart.	All-purpose. Size and texture make it choice for cooking.
Haralson	Red with tart flavor.	All-purpose. Especially good for carameled apples.
Jonathan	Small size with tart, zesty flavor. Juicy.	All-purpose. Eating fresh/ salads and baking.
McIntosh	Bright red color; rich flavor with juicy, fairly crisp texture.	All-purpose, but can become mushy when overcooked or used in pies.
Rome Beauty	Red-striped skin. Firm with mildly-tart flavor.	Excellent for baking; holds shape well.
Wealthy	Large with red/yellow streaking. Crisp and tart.	All-purpose.
Winesap	Noted for deep red color and juiciness. Rich flavor.	Excellent for both fresh eating and cooking.

Other good choices for cooking are Ben Davis, Stayman, York Imperial, Paragon, Northern Spy, Newton Pipin, Lodi, Rhode Island Greening and Yellow Transparent.

Additional good-eating choices include Gravenstein, Northern Spy, Connell Red, Fireside, Idared, Spartan, Maiden's Blush, Macoun and Opalescent.

Nutrition Information

Pillsbury's **NUTRI-CODED** system can help you in your daily food planning.** Below are guidelines:

SERVING SIZE: This has been determined as a typical serving for each recipe.

CALORIES: The amount of calories a person needs is determined by age, size and activity level. The recommended daily allowances generally are: 1800-2400 for women and children 4 to 10 years of age and 2400-2800 for men.

PROTEIN: The amount of protein needed daily is determined by age and size; the general U.S. RDA is 65 grams for adults and children of at least 4 years of age.

CARBOHYDRATE, FAT, CHOLESTEROL, SODIUM, AND POTASSIUM: Recommended Dietary Allowances (RDA) for these nutrients have not been determined; however, the carbohydrate should be adequate so the body does not burn protein for energy. The American Heart Association recommendation for those who wish to restrict dietary cholesterol is for a daily intake that is less than 100 milligrams per 1000 calories and not exceeding a total of 300 milligrams.

PERCENT U.S. RDA PER SERVING: For a nutritionally balanced diet, choose recipes which will provide 100% of the U.S. Recommended Daily Allowance for each nutrient.

Pillsbury Guidelines for Calculating the Nutrition Information:

- When the ingredient listing gives one or more options, the first ingredient listed is the one analyzed.
- When a range is given for an ingredient, the larger amount is analyzed.
- When ingredients are listed as "if desired," these ingredients are included in the nutrition information.
- Serving suggestions listed in the ingredients are calculated in the nutrition information.
- When each bread recipe is analyzed, a serving of yeast-leavened bread is a 1-oz. slice and a quick bread serving, ¹⁄₁₆ of the loaf. Recipes that vary are indicated.

Symbol Meanings:

The following symbols are used in relation to the nutrition data:

   *   Less than 2% of the nutrient
  <1   Less than one gram (or milligram) of the nutrient

Any questions regarding nutrition information in this book should be addressed to:

The Pillsbury Company
Pillsbury Center — Suite 2866
Minneapolis, Minnesota 55402

**The primary source for values used in this program is the revised Agriculture Handbook No. 8 and is only as correct and complete as the information supplies.

NOTE FOR PEOPLE WITH SPECIAL DIETARY NEEDS: CONSULT YOUR PHYSICIAN REGARDING RELIANCE ON THE NUTRITION INFORMATION IN THIS BOOK.

Every effort has been made to ensure the accuracy of this information. However, The Pillsbury Company does not guarantee its suitability for specific medically imposed diets.

Index